# BOYFRIEND
# SWEATERS

# BOYFRIEND
# SWEATERS

**19 DESIGNS FOR HIM THAT YOU'LL WANT TO WEAR**
PLUS 19 TECHNIQUES THAT HELP YOU KNIT ALMOST ANYTHING

## Bruce Weinstein
Photography by Jared Flood

POTTER
CRAFT
NEW YORK

Published in the United States by Potter Craft, an imprint of the
Crown Publishing Group, a division of Random House, Inc., New York.
www.crownpublishing.com
www.pottercraft.com

POTTER CRAFT and colophon are registered trademarks of Random
House, Inc.

Library of Congress Cataloging-in-Publication Data
Weinstein, Bruce, 1960-
   Boyfriend sweaters : 19 designs for him that you'll want to wear :
plus 19 techniques that help you knit almost anything / by Bruce
Weinstein. -- First Edition.
      pages cm
   Includes index.
   (alk. paper)
1.  Knitting--Patterns.  2.  Sweaters.  3.  Men's clothing.  I. Title.
   TT825.W452 2012
   746.43'2--dc23
                                        2012001322
ISBN 978-0-307-58712-1
eISBN 978-0-307-58713-8

Printed in China

Design by Jenny Kraemer
Photography by Jared Flood
Tech editing and schematics by Therese Chynoweth

Thanks to the Craft Yarn Council of America (www.yarnstandards.com)
for their Standard Yarn Weight System chart, which appears on page 154.

10 9 8 7 6 5 4 3 2 1

First Edition

In memory of my Grandma Hilda,
who only knit me sweaters in the patterns,
yarns, and colors I chose—at times,
against her better judgment.

# CONTENTS

**Chapter 1** ▶

## LINE AND DRAPE

**Chapter 2** ▶

## TEXTURE

# ACKNOWLEDGMENTS

Creating a sweater is a quiet activity. Alone in my studio, I look out over the woods and mountains of the lower Berkshires. Creating a knitting book, on the other hand, is the less-than-quiet product of a well-oiled, heavily manned machine. Thanks to my agent, Susan Ginsburg, who for seventeen years has helped expand my career and keep everything in perspective; editors Betty Wong and Caitlin Harpin, who combined vision with flexibility and were a dream to work with; art director Jess Morphew and book designer Jenny Kraemer, who visualized my concept in a way I couldn't even have imagined; my incredibly patient and exacting tech editor, Therese Chynoweth, who turned even my most confusing explanations into clear and concise directions; photographer Jared Flood, who can put everything in the best light; the entire production team at Potter Craft, who worked tirelessly behind the scenes to make this book happen; all the yarn manufacturers in this book, who were generous and kind even when I changed my mind about colors every other week; sample knitters Julie Himmel, Kate Belando, Denise Balvanz, Jodi Lewanda, Rosemary Keilty, Phyllis Holdaway, Pat Scully, Nancy Hand, and Jean Chung, who all overwhelm me with their talent and speed; and my partner, Mark, who gave me space and support to work on this large collection, encouraged me through all the mistakes, and who lovingly wears everything I knit for him.

# A BRIEF
# INTRODUCTION

# As long as men have had sweaters, women have worn them.

In the thirties Marlene Dietrich showed the world it was just plain sexy. In the fifties it was a sign of going steady. In the seventies it was just hard to tell men's clothes from women's—and sometimes it was hard to tell *men* from women. If you were too young to have lived through it, ask your mother who David Cassidy was. But the underlying reason women like men's fashion has always been, and continues to be, comfort. In general, men's sweaters are roomier, with less shaping. Whalebone corsets may have gone out of fashion a century ago, but women's fashion can still be uncomfortable, if not impossible to wear—just watch the red-carpet fashion show at the Oscars. Some beaded and sequined dresses weigh more than the actresses wearing them. And while most women's designs show every bump and bulge, men's fashion can hide a multitude of sins—something men have taken advantage of for decades. Men's sweaters give women the freedom to wear something comfortable and very forgiving.

So what is a boyfriend sweater exactly? It's a garment designed with the lines and colors men like, but with an unmistakable appeal to women, too. A man can wear a boyfriend sweater knit to his measurements, while a woman can wear a boyfriend sweater tailored to her size and shape or right out of his closet. A boyfriend sweater is flexible, comfortable, and most of all it's stylish on either sex. The sweaters in this book are all sized for both sexes and run the gamut from weekend casual to workday chic.

The idea for a collection of sweaters that would appeal to both men and women came from my students and from knitters I met all over the country. But I don't think they even knew they were asking for it.

When I started traveling around the U.S. teaching classes and showing the finished designs from my first book of men's patterns, women would slip on the sample sweaters and stand in front of the mirror.

"I'm making this for me," one woman would say, "In purple."

"What about adding elbow patches to the hooded sweatshirt?" another woman asked me in a class.

"Do you think this henley would look nice in bright yellow?" asked another.

There were boyfriend sweaters forming in front of my eyes, in the most classic sense: men's sweaters morphing into garments that women would also enjoy. I knew that my next collection of patterns had to appeal to both women and men right off the bat.

So you hold in your hands *Boyfriend Sweaters*—nineteen designs inspired by menswear that balance the line between colorful style and neutral simplicity so anyone will feel good in them. With tips and ideas to make each one more masculine or more feminine, most are sized from 34" (86.5cm) to 56" (142cm). Perfect for him. Perfect for her.

## How to Use this Book

*Boyfriend Sweaters* is divided into 4 sections: Line and Drape, Texture, Reversibility, and Color. Each section contains patterns that reflect the main theme and each is labeled Easy, Intermediate, or Experienced. At the beginning of each section is a small refresher on the techniques needed to complete the patterns in that section plus some helpful tips and hints to get you through just about any knitting dilemma.

## A Note About Sizing

Choosing the correct size to knit is one of the most frustrating decisions when starting a new project. As you look at sizes and finished measurements of each garment, you might be confused as to why a woman's small might be 44¼" (112.5cm) in one sweater and 42" (106.5cm) in another. The answer is that some sweaters are designed to hang more loosely than others and the overall look has been taken into consideration in the sizing. So if you normally wear a medium, that is the size you should knit. But do take a look at what the finished measurements of that garment are going to be. If it's meant to fit snugly, but you prefer something with more drape, you should feel free to go up one or two sizes. And if my version of your size seems way too big for your taste, it's okay to knit the sweater in a smaller size.

# 1.

# **LINE** AND **DRAPE**

If you or the man you're knitting for likes things simple, these projects will be perfect. They're all basic designs with clean lines and classic drape. We're keeping it boxy, square, and muted, with a few simple cables. Here you'll find something you both might throw on for a weekend walk in the woods or a Saturday night movie. Make it for him, borrow it from his closet, or just make one for yourself.

# READING PATTERNS,
## CHARTS, AND SCHEMATICS

You would never start cooking without reading through an entire recipe. The worst thing in cooking is when you turn the page and find some surprise instructions. For instance, after mixing your marinade, you find that your chicken needs to soak at least four hours, but dinner is in two hours. Or you've baked your potatoes to make gnocchi, only to find that you need to put them through a ricer when they're cool. You don't have a ricer and what's worse, you don't even know what one is. These kinds of surprises come up in knitting as well. In patterns, as in recipes, you need to know what's going to happen before you get to it. Do you have the right tools at home—the right size needles, buttons, zippers, stitch holders, scissors, or other notions that the pattern requires? Do you know what all the abbreviations mean? Do you

understand all the techniques you need to finish the project? Read through the pattern before starting a project. Better yet, read through the pattern at the yarn store, where supplies are at hand and experts are onsite to make sure your questions are answered before you start to knit.

## SIZE IS EVERYTHING

Most patterns list both finished garment and chest sizes. Chest sizes are measured with a tape measure around the chest (or bust) with a T-shirt or bra on. If only one size is listed make sure you know whether it's a chest size or a finished garment size. A man with a 44" (112cm) chest needs a 48" (122cm) sweater. Those extra 4" (10cm) are called ease, and while some men like sweaters that fit tighter, with less ease, 3–4" (7.5cm-10cm) are usually a good call. For a cardigan, err on the large size, that is 4" (10cm) or even 5" (12.5cm) of ease if the guy likes to wear heavy shirts or another sweater underneath. The best way to make sure a sweater fits a man the way he likes it is to measure a sweater he already has and knit the new one in the same size. Just be sure to measure the same style sweater that you are creating, e.g., raglan, set-in sleeve, dropped-shoulder, etc.

Ease for a boyfriend sweater on a woman is tricky. A boyfriend sweater is meant to look a bit oversized on a woman, so you should consider adding 1" (2.5cm) more ease than you would normally add for a standard woman's sweater. In the end, it's all about personal style and comfort, so the best advice I can give is to drop by the men's department of any store and try on a few sweaters. Bring your tape measure and measure the ones you like. Then you'll know exactly how much ease you prefer in a sweater that's shaped for a man.

Sizes offered in any given pattern are listed up front, in a row of numbers with all but the first inside of parentheses. This format follows throughout the pattern. So if your size is the first number inside the parentheses, then you will always follow the directions using the first number inside the parentheses as you knit. It's a good idea to circle this number (in

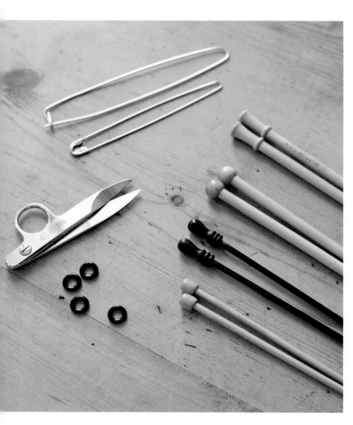

pencil) throughout the entire pattern to avoid any mistakes later on.

# READING SCHEMATICS

Schematics are one of the best tools a knitter has to see if she or he is getting all the parts right. These drawings show you how each part of the sweater will look and how long and wide each section is. The schematic will also list sizes as a series of numbers (all but the first in parentheses). Circle the ones you need (in pencil) to follow before you start so you can easily find your size when referring to the diagram. If you're making adjustments to the pattern for someone taller or shorter, make sure to circle the appropriate length you're looking for. To keep the sleeves and body fitting together properly, make all your height adjustments to the body and sleeves between the armholes and the waist/cuffs.

# UNDERSTANDING CHARTS

Charts are usually included for cables, colorwork, or other interesting stitchery. Each box in that chart represents one stitch. (In double knitting each box represents two stitches, but that's a unique situation—see page 92.) Each horizontal row on the chart represents one row of stitches. Most charts are read from right to left for right-side rows and left to right for wrong-side rows. A chart for knitting in the round will be read from right to left on every round.

Every chart will have a legend below it to show what all the symbols (or lack of symbols) mean in each box. Many designers use different symbols, so don't take this legend for granted. Make sure you're following what the designer intended.

Sometimes different sizes begin and end on different places on the chart. So look for any markings that show you where your size falls on the chart and where any repeats will happen.

Even experienced knitters have trouble with charts when working sleeves and other shaped pieces.

## WRITING IN YOUR BOOKS

I encourage you to write notes, tips, and other tidbits you've learned while making any project so you'll remember it for the next time. But use a pencil for things like circling sizes since you're likely to make a different size next time. All those circles, in ink, can get confusing.

That's because they require increases that expand the design beyond the sides of the chart. Patterns will say to work new stitches into established pattern as you increase. The more complicated the stitch or colorwork is, the more likely the designer will indicate on the chart how to add new stitches into the existing pattern, to make your life easier. If it's not done for you and you can't figure that out in your head (most of us can't), take a ruler and pencil and extend your chart out, creating empty boxes on either side. Then fill in those boxes, expanding the design so you'll know exactly how to incorporate the pattern into the increased stitches.

# GETTING GAUGE

Gauge may be the most important word in knitting. Without a gauge swatch you never know if your finished garment will be the right size. Students tell me all the time that they hate knitting gauge swatches. Many think it's a waste of good knitting time. But in fact, starting a sweater *without* doing a gauge swatch is a waste of good knitting time. If I spend thirty hours knitting a sweater, I want to make sure it's going to fit when I'm done.

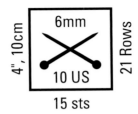

4", 10cm
6mm
10 US
21 Rows
15 sts

An icon like this appears on nearly every skein of yarn. In this case it means that the manufacturer thinks this yarn looks best at 15 stitches and 21 rows over 4 inches. The needle size required to get this gauge is only a manufacturer's suggestion, in this case a size U.S. 10. It's just a suggestion because some of us knit more loosely or more tightly than others. I knit loosely, so if I follow the manufacturer's suggested needle size, my gauge is going to be off—I will get fewer stitches over 4" (10cm) than they say I should get. And that can easily turn my 40" (101.5cm) sweater into a 44" (112cm) sweater. Start your gauge swatch with the needles suggested and then go up or down a size depending on your results. Remember, if you are getting too many stitches per inch, go up a needle size. If you're getting too few stitches per inch, go down a needle size. Keep trying different needles until you get the exact number of stitches per inch the pattern requires.

Knitting in the round makes doing a gauge swatch a little more difficult. Because unless otherwise indicated, gauge swatches are knit in stockinette stitch—alternating rows of knit stitches with rows of purl stitches. But knitting in the round creates stockinette fabric with no purling—all you do is knit. And if you knit a flat piece of stockinette you won't have an accurate gauge because your tension may be looser when you purl. So there are two ways to get an accurate gauge in the round.

▶ Knit your gauge on 9" (23cm) circular needles. You'll knit a small tube giving you a perfect gauge but wasting a lot of time and yarn.

▶ Knit a small swatch on two double-pointed needles. Cast on 24 stitches to one double-pointed needle. Knit this row across a second double-pointed needle. Don't turn the knitting. Slide the

knitting from the left side to the right side of the same needle. Drape the yarn across the back from the left side to the right side so that the yarn is in the proper place to start knitting across the same row you just knit. With the right side facing you, a second row of knitting will create stockinette stitch. When you finish this row, repeat the process. You will end up with a flat piece of stockinette knitting with yarn draped across the back in rows.

How you measure your gauge swatch is just as important as how you knit it. No matter what technique you use, always knit a swatch least 6" (15cm) square to get an accurate measurement. This will allow you to measure your 4" (10cm) section with a little room to spare. Ends and edges can often misshape or curl and throw off a measurement. Also, take the swatch off the needles before measuring, as the needles can also pull on the knitting. If you plan on blocking your finished garment be sure to block the gauge swatch. And don't forget to measure your swatch in two or three places to make sure your measurement is correct.

# INCREASING
## AND DECREASING

Unless otherwise indicated in a pattern, all increases should be done as knit front and back (kfb) if the increase occurs before a knit stitch, and purl front and back (pfb) if the increase occurs before a purl stitch.

To **knit front and back**, insert your right-hand needle into the next stitch on the left-hand needle in the normal fashion as if to knit. Wrap or grab your working yarn with your right-hand needle and pull the working yarn through to the front but do not slip the left-hand stitch off the needle. Pull a little extra slack on the working yarn with your right-hand needle and then insert it into the back of the stitch you just knit into. Wrap or grab the working yarn again and pull it through to the front. Now drop the left-hand stitch off the needle, and you have created an extra stitch.

To **purl front and back**, insert your right-hand needle into the next stitch on the left-hand needle in the normal fashion as if to purl. Wrap or grab your working yarn with your right-hand needle and pull the working yarn through to the back but do not drop the old stitch off the left-hand needle. Pull some extra slack on the working yarn with your right-hand needle, then insert the needle as if to purl into the back of the stitch you just purled in the normal way. Wrap or grab your working yarn and pull it to the back. Drop the old stitch from the left-hand needle.

Traditionally, when you decrease on the front, or right side (RS) of the fabric, you knit two stitches together (k2tog) on the left edge, and slip, slip, knit (ssk) on the right edge.

**K2tog** is a right-slanting decrease and is done by inserting the right-hand needle into the first two stitches on the left needle together, as if to knit, starting with the second stitch. Now wrap or grab your working yarn and bring it through both stitches together.

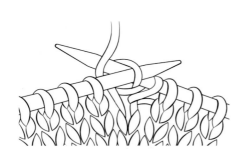

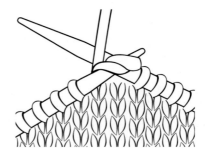

**Slip, slip, knit** is a left-slanting decrease and is done by slipping the first stitch to be decreased on the left-hand needle, as if to knit, followed by the second stitch on the left-hand needle, as if to knit. As you slip each to the right-hand needle you are flipping them around so they now face the back (a).

Insert the left-hand needle back into both stitches together from left to right, wrap or grab your yarn with your right-hand needle and knit both stitches together (b).

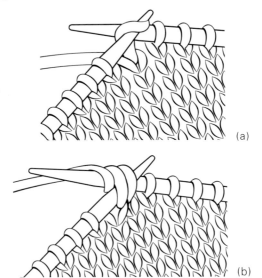

(a)

(b)

Decreasing on the back, or wrong, side (WS) is done by purling two stitches together (p2tog) on the left edge and slip, slip, purl (ssp) on the right edge. **P2tog** is done by inserting the right-hand needle into the first 2 stitches on the left-hand needle from right to left, then wrapping or grabbing the working yarn and purling the 2 stitches together.

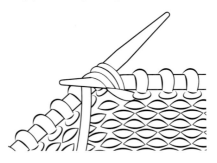

To **slip, slip, purl, slip** the first stitch from the left-hand needle as if to knit, then the second stitch from the left-hand needle as if to knit. As you slip each to the right-hand needle you are flipping them around so they now face the back. Insert the left-hand needle back into both stitches together from left to right, and remove your right hand needle. Insert the right-hand needle back into both stitches together, as if to purl from the back. Wrap or grab your yarn with your right-hand needle and purl both stitches together.

### A Note About Increasing on Sleeves

Almost all sleeves require increases to get from the diameter of your wrist up to the diameter of your upper arm. For sleeves knit from the top down, decreases are made in order to get them to fit properly. Unless otherwise indicated in the pattern, always make sleeve increases or decreases 1 stitch in from the edge. This will allow you to make a

smooth seam along the sleeve with the increases/decreases appearing as a tiny design element up the length of the sleeve.

# PICKING UP STITCHES

You can start a new piece of knitting along the edge of a previously knit piece using several methods. With all these techniques, you will use an empty needle to bring loops of new yarn through existing stitches, then knit those loops.

### Picking Up Stitches Across a Bound-off Edge

Hold your knitting with the bound-off edge facing up and unless otherwise called for, the right side facing you. Starting at the upper right corner of the work, insert your needle into the middle of the V that forms the first stitch in the row directly under the bound-off edge. With a new ball of yarn, wrap the needle as if to knit and pull it through the old stitch. Insert your needle into the middle of the V of the next stitch directly to the left of the previous stitch, wrap the needle, and bring the new loop through the old stitch. Continue across the row picking up one stitch for each bound-off stitch. Turn your work and purl back. You now have your first row. The trick of picking up a perfectly straight line of stitches is to make sure you insert your empty needle into the stitch directly to the left of the one you just did. Don't go down a row or into the bound off-edging above.

### Picking Up Stitches Along the Side Edge

This technique will build new stitches perpendicular to the old ones. Turn your work sideways so the edge you want to pick up from is on top. Before you begin, examine the knitting. The Vs that make up the stitches are running left to right instead of up and down. You will start again at the upper right-hand corner but instead of inserting your needle into the middle of the V that makes up the top right-hand stitch, you will insert the needle below this sideways V, into the space between this V and the V in the row just below it. Wrap your needle and pull your new stitch forward between these 2 rows. Continue down the row, inserting your needle into the space between the stitches on the first and second rows. Staying between these rows will give you a clean, straight edge. When you get to the end, turn, and purl back or follow the stitch directions in your pattern.

### Picking Up Stitches Along a Curve

If you are picking up stitches along a curved edge you may need to follow the rules for a picking up stitches along bound-off edge and a side edge all in one row. Patterns often tell you how many stitches to pick up in a given length of a curved edge and require you to space them out evenly. Sometimes this means skipping a V or crowding stitches in between Vs. In this situation, use your best judgment. If you don't like the way the first row looks when it's done, you can rip it out and try again.

# SEWING IN ZIPPERS

Sewing in a zipper can be frustrating, but there are tricks that help you get it right the first time.

- Start with a custom-length zipper. There are many places to order these, but my favorite is A. Feibusch Corp., on New York City's Lower East Side (or online at www.zipperstop.com).

- Choose a thread that is close to your sweater color so that it disappears into the knitting.

- Work on a large, flat, clean space—the dining room table works perfectly.

- Sew the zipper in before sewing the rest of the sweater together. But sew the shoulder seams first, in order to put on a collar, if the collar is part of the zipper arrangement.

Arrange the two front pieces facing down, lining them up exactly. With the zipper fully zipped up and with the zipper pulls facing down, place the zipper teeth into the seam where the two pieces of knitting line up. Align the top and bottom of the zipper with the top and bottom of the knitting and set the zipper in place, using pins every inch or two.

If you are sewing by hand, use a backstitch, keeping the stitches close to the teeth and pulling out the pins as you go. As you sew, keep the stitches in a straight line between a row of knit stitches so that the thread is not visibly crossing over any Vs of the knit stitches on the right side. When the entire length is sewn in, whipstitch the edge of the zipper tape down the backside, only through the loops of the knit stitches on the wrong side.

## Machine Sewing a Zipper

Machine sewing makes a sturdier connection, but it is usually visible on the right side of the sweater. It also requires you to place your pins farther away from the zipper teeth or you run the risk of sewing over them and breaking your sewing machine's needle. If your sweater has a ribbed edge by the

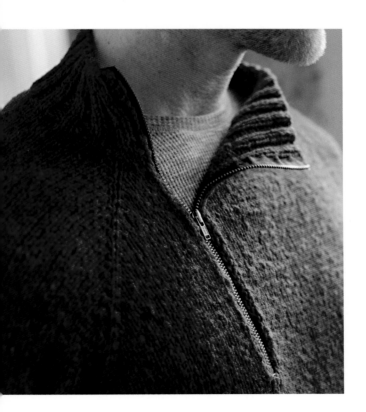

## BACKSTITCH

Thread your needle, tie a small knot in the thread, and pull it through your fabric, from back to front. Sewing from right to left, insert your needle from front to back and make a ½" (13mm) stitch. Next, insert your needle from back to front, ¼" (6mm) to the right from where you are—you have gone back directly to the middle of the first stitch, hence the "backstitch." Insert the needle from front to back ½" (13mm) to the left and repeat.

zipper, you can guide the sweater under the sewing machine foot so that the line of sewn stitches is hidden between the knit rib ridges. Make sure you change the standard foot to a zipper foot on your machine. Sewing by machine will still require you to whipstitch the zipper tape edge by hand on the back side of your fabric.

# SEWING SEAMS

Tight seams are the bedrock of a good sweater. Even the most beautiful knitting can be lost behind sloppy finishing. But seams scare many knitters. That's why my classes on seamless sweaters fill up faster than classes on sewing proper seams. But seams are easier than most knitters realize, if you start with the right tools—in this case, a yarn needle or blunt-tip tapestry needle. Regular tapestry needles are sharp and can break your yarn as you go. Also, grab a pair of reading glasses even if you don't need them for reading. The magnification they offer makes it easier to see where to insert your needle when seaming. Plan on sewing your seam with the same yarn you used for knitting the sweater. If it's a very heavy yarn *and* it's plied, it's possible to untwist the ply and use only half of the threads for a less bulky seam. If your yarn is loosely spun it might break as you pull it to tighten seams. In this case, use a stronger yarn of the same weight and color as your garment.

There's a benefit to working on the right side of the garment, which is that you can see how it's coming along with every pull of the yarn.

### Sewing Rows to Rows
Sewing body and sleeve seams on the right side means you will be joining two side edges together—sometimes called joining rows to rows. Place the knitting right side facing you on your work surface and line the pieces up so that they are touching where you want the seam to be. The rows on the left side will line up exactly with the rows on the right side. The first stitch on each side is your selvedge stitch, or the stitch that will be incorporated into your seam. To see these stitches, pull the edges of your fabric with your fingers and you'll see a line of horizontal bars that runs between the first and second stitch in each row. That horizontal bar is what you're aiming for. Insert the needle under the first horizontal bar on the side opposite your tail. Pull the yarn through. Cross over the top of the knitting and slip the needle under the first horizontal bar on the other side. Pull the yarn through without tightening it all the way—leave ½" (13mm) of yarn exposed. Insert the needle under the second horizontal bar on the opposite side but do not tighten it—again, leave ½" (13mm) of yarn draped over the seam. Repeat this process until you have sewn about 1" (2.5cm) of stitches. Gently tug the yarn to pull these stitches tight. The ½" (13mm) bits of slack will disappear as the two sides come together in a neat seam. Continue in this manner until the entire seam is sewn.

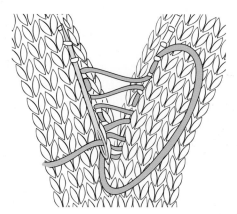

### Sewing Stitches to Stitches

Joining cast-off edges together at a shoulder seam is sometimes referred to as joining stitches to stitches. The technique is the same as joining rows to rows, only you will be slipping the yarn needle under the V of each stitch in the row directly next to the cast-off edge. Line up the pieces, right side facing you, with both cast-off edges touching. Thread the yarn needle with one of the tails left from casting off and slip the yarn needle under the first V just below the cast-on edge on the side opposite your tail. Cross over, leaving ½" (13mm) of yarn draped over the seam, and slip the yarn needle under the first V (first stitch) on the other side. Repeat this process across the row, tightening the yarn and pulling the seam together every inch or so.

Sometimes you will sew stitches to rows, that is, a side edge to a cast-off edge. In that case, simply slip the needle under the horizontal bar on one side and under the V on the other side.

# CABLES

Cables are one of the most versatile and distinctive design elements in knitting. Entire books are devoted to its praise. If you've never done a cable before, you need to know that cables are a small group of stitches knit out of order. Imagine you're knitting along a row of 24 stitches in stockinette

> ## WHICH WAY IS YOUR CABLE LEANING?
>
> If you held your cable needle with those 3 forgotten stitches in the front while you knit stitches 13, 14, and 15, your cable will lean to the left. If you held it in the back, your cable will lean to the right. Every pattern or cable chart will tell you where to position the cable needle.

and you just finished stitch 9. To form a 6-stitch cable here you need to skip stitch numbers 10, 11, and 12, knitting stitches 13, 14, and 15 first. Get stitch numbers 10, 11, and 12 out of the way by slipping them to a cable needle or a small double-pointed needle (a). Hold them out of the way (the pattern will indicate whether to hold them behind your knitting or in front of it) and knit numbers 13, 14, and 15 (b).

To knit stitches 10, 11, and 12 after the fact, let go of your left-hand needle and pick up the cable needle with those 3 forgotten stitches on them. Pull this needle over to the left and slide the stitches to the far right end of it where you can knit them onto your right-hand needle (c). After you've knitted them, drop the empty cable needle, pick up the left-hand needle with stitches 16 through 24 on it, and you're good to go. You do not knit these stitches out of order on every row. The pattern will tell you how often to repeat it, typically every 4th, 6th, or 8th row.

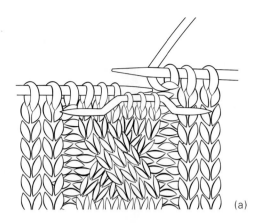

(a)

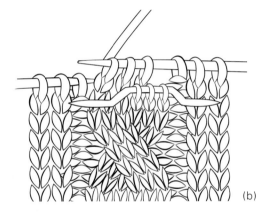

(b)

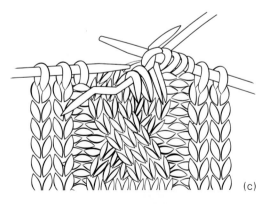

(c)

## DOUBLE POINTS VS. CABLE NEEDLES

Cable needles have a small dip in them to keep your stitches from sliding off. And they're usually shorter than regular double-pointed needles, making them easier to manipulate. But cable needles usually come in only 3 sizes: small, medium, and large. Using a short double-pointed needle lets you use the same size needle as the rest of the knit piece, but they're more cumbersome. There's a trade-off in each, so try both and use whichever one feels best for you.

# **Off-Center** Half-Zip Mock Turtle

This might just become your favorite sweatshirt-style sweater. Nothing looks better than this classic with a pair of jeans or khakis. The off-center zipper adds a stylish, unexpected detail, and knitting in the round makes it a snap to finish.

**Skill Level** ▶ Easy

**Finished Measurements**

| Woman's Size | Man's Size | Bust/Chest | Length |
|---|---|---|---|
| S | XS | 39" (99cm) | 28¼" (72cm) |
| M | S | 43½" (110.5cm) | 28¾" (73cm) |
| L | M | 47¼" (120cm) | 29" (74cm) |
| XL | L | 50¾" (129cm) | 29¾" (75.5cm) |
| XXL | XL | 55½" (141cm) | 30¼" (77cm) |
| XXXL | XXL | 59" (150cm) | 30¾" (78cm) |

If only one number is used, it applies to all sizes.

## Materials
- Brooklyn Tweed Shelter (100% Targhee-Columbia wool, each approximately 1¾ oz [50g] and 140 yd [128m]; 9 (10, 11, 12, 13, 14) skeins in color 01 Long Johns, (4) medium
- Size U.S. 7 (4.5 mm) 36" (91cm) circular needle, or size needed to obtain gauge
- Size U.S. 7 (4.5mm) double-pointed needles, set of 5
- stitch markers
- 10" (25.5cm) zipper
- Blunt-tip yarn needle

## Gauge
19½ stitches and 28 rows = 4" (10cm) in stockinette stitch
To save time, take time to check gauge.

## Stitch Pattern
K2, P2 Rib *(multiple of 4 stitches)*

### In the Round:
ROUND 1 (RS): *K2, p2; repeat from * to the end.
Repeat Round 1 for the pattern.

### Flat:
ROW 1 (RS): * K2, p2; repeat from * to the end.
ROW 2 (WS): * P2, k2; repeat from * to the end.

## Note
This sweater is worked from the top down, beginning at the neck rib.

# Body

With the circular needle, cast on 100 (104, 108, 112, 116, 120) stitches. Do not join.

Work in the rib pattern until the piece measures 2¼" (5.5cm), ending with a right-side row.

**NEXT ROW (WS):** Set up the stitches for the raglan yoke as follows: P4 (5, 6, 7, 8, 9) for the right front, pm, p14 for the right sleeve, pm, p37 (39, 41, 43, 45, 47) for the back, pm, p14 for the left sleeve, pm, p31 (32, 33, 34, 35, 36) for the left front.

**INCREASE ROW (RS):** *Knit to 1 stitch before the marker, knit into the front and back of the next stitch, slip the marker, knit into the front and back of the next stitch; repeat from * 3 times more, then knit to the end—108 (112, 116, 120, 124, 128) stitches.

Continue in stockinette stitch and repeat the increase row every right-side row 20 (26, 30, 34, 40, 43) times more, then every 4 rows 6 (4, 3, 2, 0, 0) times—316 (352, 380, 408, 444, 472) stitches. Work 4 (4, 2, 2, 0, 0) rows even. *At the same time,* when the piece measures 10" (25.5cm) from the cast-on edge, join the piece to begin working in the round. Place a marker to indicate the beginning and end of your rounds.

Note: if you have the chance to slip this on your man, or on yourself, this is a good time to do so. Make sure the raglan length comes to approximately 1" (2.5cm) below the underarm. For most people the lengths indicated will be sufficient. For people with long torsos, you may need to knit even for up to an additional ½" (13mm) to 1" (2.5cm).

## DIVIDE BODY AND SLEEVES

Removing all markers as you work except for the beginning of the round marker, knit to the first marker, place the next 68 (76, 82, 88, 96, 102) stitches on a piece of scrap yarn for the left sleeve, cast on 5 (6, 7, 8, 9, 10) stitches for the underarm, knit to the next marker for the back, place the next 68 (76, 82, 88, 96, 102) stitches on a piece of scrap yarn for the right sleeve, cast on 5 (6, 7, 8, 9, 10) stitches for the underarm, knit to the end of the round—190 (212, 230, 248, 270, 288) stitches remain on the needle.

Continue even in stockinette stitch until the body measures 13½" (34.5cm) from the underarm.

Change to the K2, P2 Rib pattern and decrease 2 (0, 2, 0, 2, 0) stitches evenly spaced across the round—188 (212, 228, 248, 268, 288) stitches remain. Continue even until the rib measures 2½" (6.5cm). Bind off all stitches in the pattern.

## Sleeves (Make 2)

Place the 68 (76, 82, 88, 96, 102) stitches for one sleeve on double-pointed needles, or the 36" (91cm) circular needle if you are using the Magic Loop method. Begin at the center of the cast-on underarm stitches, and pick up and knit 3 (3, 4, 4, 5, 5) stitches, knit the sleeve stitches, then pick up and knit 2 (3, 3, 4, 4, 5) stitches along the remaining cast-on underarm stitches—73 (82, 89, 96, 105, 112)

stitches. Place a marker for the beginning of the round.

Knit 6 rounds even (all sizes).

**DECREASE ROUND:** K2, k2tog, knit to the last 4 stitches, ssk, k2—71 (80, 87, 94, 103, 110) stitches remain.

Repeat the decrease round every 10 (8, 7, 7, 6, 6) rounds 4 (5, 16, 5, 12, 2) times, then every 9 (7, 0, 6, 5, 5) rounds 8 (10, 0, 13, 9, 21) times–47 (50, 55, 58, 61, 64) stitches remain. The sleeve should measure about 16½ (16¾, 17¼, 17¼, 17¾, 17¾)" (42 [42.5, 44, 44, 45, 45] cm) from the underarm.

Change to the k2, p2 rib pattern, and decrease 3 (2, 3, 2, 1, 0) stitch(es) evenly spaced on the first round—44 (48, 52, 56, 60, 64) stitches remain. Continue even until the rib measures 2" (5cm). Bind off all stitches in the pattern.

## Finishing

Weave in all ends. Block all pieces lightly.

Sew in the zipper (see page 20).

Sew in the zipper (see page 20).

---

**MAKE IT MORE FEMININE**

Look for a zipper with nylon or plastic teeth for a less masculine look. For a subtle feminine touch buy a zipper with white or other contrasting color tape—that is the fabric along the sides of the teeth. It will stand out as a decorative bit.

---

## OFF-CENTER HALF-ZIP MOCK TURTLE **SCHEMATIC**

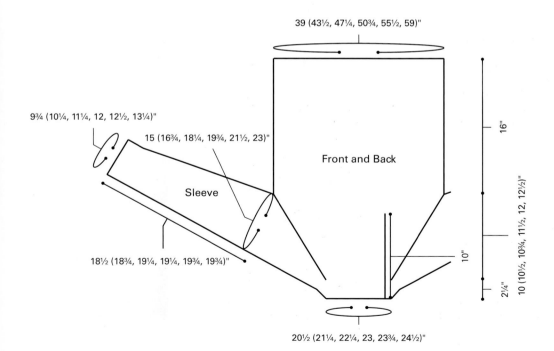

39 (43½, 47¼, 50¾, 55½, 59)"

9¾ (10¼, 11¼, 12, 12½, 13¼)"

15 (16¾, 18¼, 19¾, 21½, 23)"

Front and Back

Sleeve

16"

10 (10½, 10¾, 11½, 12, 12½)"

10"

2¼"

18½ (18¾, 19¼, 19¼, 19¾, 19¾)"

20½ (21¼, 22¼, 23, 23¾, 24½)"

# **Oversized** Turtleneck

The extra-wide collar on this sweater is übercomfortable, and the dropped shoulder seams are at once stylish, subtle, and sophisticated. This sweater is supposed to be roomier than most, so if you're unsure about a size, make sure you account for all that built-in ease.

**Skill Level** ▶ Intermediate

**Finished Measurements**

| Woman's Size | Man's Size | Bust/Chest | Length |
|---|---|---|---|
| S | XS | 40" (101.5cm) | 28½" (72cm) |
| M | S | 44" (112cm) | 29" (74cm) |
| L | M | 47½" (120.5cm) | 29½" (75cm) |
| XL | L | 52" (132cm) | 30" (76cm) |
| XXL | XL | 56" (142cm) | 30½" (77.5cm) |
| XXXL | XXL | 60" (152.5cm) | 31" (79cm) |

If only one number is used, it applies to all sizes.

**Materials**
- Rowan Felted Tweed Aran (50% merino wool, 25% alpaca, 25% viscose, each approximately 1¾ oz [50g] and 95 yd [87m]), 15 (16, 18, 19, 21, 22) balls in color 724 Heather, (**4**) medium
- One pair size U.S. 7 (4.5mm) knitting needles, or size needed to obtain gauge
- Size U.S. 7 (4.5mm) 16" (40cm) circular needle
- Stitch holder
- Blunt-tip yarn needle
- Stitch marker

**Gauge**
17 stitches and 25 rows = 4" (10cm) in stockinette stitch
To save time, take time to check gauge.

**Stitch Pattern**
K2, P2 Rib *(multiple of 4 + 2 stitches)*
ROW 1 (RS): K2, *p2, k2; repeat from * to the end.
ROW 2 (WS): P2, *k2, p2; repeat from * to the end.
Repeat Rows 1 and 2 for the pattern.

> ## SLIPPING THE FIRST STITCH

Many knitters like to slip the first stitch of each row for a clean edge. This is creates a neat chain selvedge edge that is easy to see, but it also makes it harder to create a smooth, tight seam. I don't recommend slipping the first stitch in a row unless the pattern specifically requests that you do so. In this sweater, slipping the first stitch of each row will make it difficult to sew the shoulders seams and set in the sleeves.

## Back

With the straight needles, cast on 86 (94, 102, 110, 118, 126) stitches.

Work in the K2, P2 Rib pattern until the piece measures 3" (7.5cm), ending with a wrong-side row and increase 1 (1, 1, 3, 3, 3) stitch(es) on the last row—87 (95, 103, 113, 121, 129) stitches.

Change to stockinette stitch and work even until the piece measures 18" (45.5cm) from the cast-on edge, ending with a wrong-side row.

### SHAPE ARMHOLES

Bind off 2 (2, 3, 4, 4, 5) stitches at the beginning of the next 2 rows, then 2 stitches at the beginning of the next 2 rows—79 (87, 93, 101, 109, 115) stitches remain.

Work 2 rows even. Bind off 2 stitches at the beginning of the next 2 rows—75 (83, 89, 97, 105, 111) stitches remain.

Repeat the last 4 rows 0 (1, 2, 3, 4, 5) time(s) more—75 (79, 81, 85, 89, 91) stitches remain.

Continue even until the armhole measures 8½ (9, 9½, 9½, 10, 10½)" (21.5 [23, 24, 24, 25.5, 26.5] cm), ending with a wrong-side row.

### SHAPE SHOULDERS AND NECK

Read the entire section before knitting—the neck shaping instructions are followed by armhole shaping which are to be done simultaneously.

NEXT ROW (RS): Work 33 (34, 34, 36, 38, 38) stitches and put the remaining 42 (45, 47, 49, 51, 53) stitches on a holder. Turn and work each side separately.

## Right shoulder

Bind off 3 stitches at the beginning of the next wrong-side row, then 2 stitches at the beginning of the following 2 wrong-side rows to shape the neck.

NEXT ROW (RS): Knit to the last 2 stitches, k2tog. Repeat the neck shaping decrease on the next 0 (1, 1, 1, 1, 1) right-side row(s). At the same time, when the armhole measures 9 (9½, 10, 10½, 11, 11½)" (23 [24, 25.5, 26.5, 28, 29] cm), continue the neck shaping decrease and increase 1 stitch at the armhole edge every RS row 5 times—30 (30, 30, 32, 34, 34) stitches remain when all the shaping is complete. Note: Depending on your size, you may not decrease the neck and increase the armhole on more than one or two RS rows at the same time.

Continue even until the armhole measures 11 (11½, 12, 12½, 13, 13½)" (28 [29, 30.5, 32, 33, 34.5] cm), ending with a wrong-side row.

Bind off the remaining stitches.

## Left shoulder

With the right-side facing, place the held stitches onto a needle. Join the yarn and bind off the center 9 (11, 13, 13, 13, 15) stitches, then knit to the end—33 (34, 34, 36, 38, 38) stitches remain.

NEXT ROW (WS): Purl.

Bind off 3 stitches at the beginning of the next right-side row, then 2 stitches at the beginning of the following 2 right-side rows to shape the neck.

NEXT ROW (WS): Purl to the last 2 stitches, p2tog. Repeat the neck shaping decrease on the next 0 (1, 1, 1, 1, 1) wrong-side row(s). At the same time, when the armhole measures 9 (9½, 10, 10½, 11, 11½)" (23 [24, 25.5, 26.5,

28, 29] cm), continue the neck shaping decrease and increase 1 stitch at the armhole edge every RS row 5 times–30 (30, 30, 32, 34, 34) stitches remain when all the shaping is complete. Note: Depending on your size, you may not decrease the neck and increase the armhole on more than one or two RS rows at the same time.

Continue even until the armhole measures 11 (11½, 12, 12½, 13, 13½)" (28 [29, 30.5, 32, 33, 34.5] cm), ending with a wrong-side row.

Bind off the remaining stitches.

## Front

Work the same as the Back until the armhole measures 6½ (7, 7½, 8, 8½, 9)" (16.5 [18, 19, 20.5, 21.5, 23] cm), ending with a wrong-side row. Note: the back armhole is deeper than the front to accommodate the unusual shoulder shaping.

### SHAPE SHOULDERS AND NECK
Bind off 2 stitches at the beginning of the next 10 (10, 10, 6, 6, 6) rows—55 (59, 61, 73, 77, 79) stitches remain.

NEXT ROW (RS): Bind off 2 stitches at beginning of row, k19 (20, 20, 26, 28, 28), turn leaving the remaining 34 (37, 39, 45, 47, 49) stitches on a stitch holder. Work each side separately.

## Left front

Read the entire section before knitting—the shoulder shaping continues as the neck is being shaped.

Bind off 2 stitches at the beginning of the next 4 (4, 4, 4, 2, 2) right-side rows, then 3 stitches at the beginning of the next 1 (1, 1, 3, 5, 5) right-side row(s). At the same time, bind off 3 stitches at the beginning of the next wrong-side row, 2 stitches at the beginning of the next 2 wrong-side rows, then 1 stitch at the beginning of the next 1 (2, 2, 2, 2, 2) wrong-side row(s).

Break yarn.

## Right front

With right-side facing, place the held stitches back onto the needles. Join yarn and bind off the center 13 (15, 17, 17, 17, 19) stitches, knit to the end—21 (22, 22, 28, 30, 30) stitches remain.

Read the entire section before knitting—the shoulder shaping

continues as the neck is being shaped.

Bind off 2 stitches at the beginning of the next 4 (4, 4, 4, 2, 2) wrong-side rows, then 3 stitches at the beginning of the next 1 (1, 1, 3, 5, 5) wrong-side row(s). At the same time, bind off 3 stitches at the beginning of the next right-side row, 2 stitches at the beginning of the next 2 right-side rows, then 1 stitch at the beginning of the next 1 (2, 2, 2, 2, 2) right-side row(s).

Break yarn.

## Sleeves (Make 2)

With the straight needles, cast on 42 (46, 46, 50, 50, 54) stitches.

Work in the K2, P2 Rib pattern until the piece measures 3" (7.5cm) from the cast-on edge, ending with a wrong-side row

and increase 1 stitch on the last row—43 (47, 47, 51, 51, 55) stitches.

Change to stockinette stitch and increase 1 stitch at each end of every 4 rows 0 (0, 0, 0, 4, 4) times, every 6 rows 8 (8, 14, 14, 12, 12) times, then every 8 rows 4 (4, 0, 0, 0, 0) times—67 (71, 75, 79, 83, 87) stitches.

Work even until the piece measures 17 (17, 17½, 17½, 18, 18)" (43 [43, 44.5, 44.5, 45.5, 45.5]cm) from the cast-on edge, ending with a wrong-side row.

### SHAPE CAP
Bind off 2 (2, 3, 4, 4, 5) stitches at the beginning of the next 2 rows—63 (67, 69, 71, 75, 77) stitches remain.

**NEXT ROW (RS):** K2, k2tog, knit to the last 3 stitches, ssk, k1—61 (65, 67, 69, 73, 75) stitches remain.

**NEXT ROW (WS):** Purl.

Repeat the last 2 rows 5 (7, 7, 9, 9, 11) more times—51 (51, 53, 51, 55, 53) stitches remain.

**NEXT ROW (RS):** K1, k2tog twice, knit to the last 5 stitches, k2tog twice, k1—47 (47, 49, 47, 51, 49) stitches remain.

**NEXT ROW (WS):** Purl.

Repeat the last 2 rows 8 more times—15 (15, 17, 15, 19, 17) stitches remain.

Bind off the remaining stitches.

## Finishing
Weave in all ends. Block all pieces to the finished measurements.

### SEW SHOULDER SEAMS
The shoulder seams form diagonal lines, angling down the front of the sweater toward the armhole, creating a mini mock raglan. Sew these two edges together from the wrong side, sewing

rows to rows, so the seam is visible on the right side.

### SEW IN SLEEVES
Since the shoulder slopes toward the front, it is not obvious how the sleeve sets in. Place the Front and Back together so the bottom edges of the armholes meet. Place a pin or marker in the armhole edges at the folded edge at the top of each armhole so the seams are at the back of the armholes. Pin the sleeves into the armholes with the center of the top edge at the marker for the shoulder. Sew in the sleeves.

Sew the side and sleeve seams.

## Collar
With the circular needle, begin at the right Back neck edge, join the yarn, and pick up and knit 84 (92, 96, 96, 100, 104) stitches along the neck edge. Join to work in the round. Place a marker for the beginning of the round.

**ROUND 1:** *K2, p2; repeat from * to the end.

Repeat the last round until the collar measures 8" (20.5cm). Bind off all stitches in the rib pattern.

---

┌─ **MAKE IT MORE NEUTRAL**

If the guy getting this sweater objects to the exposed seams, sew the slanted "shoulder" seams together using the right-side invisible seam method (page 21) for a simpler look.

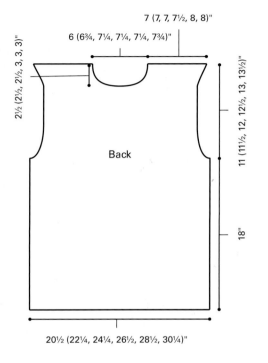

7 (7, 7, 7½, 8, 8)"

6 (6¾, 7¼, 7¼, 7¼, 7¾)"

2½ (2½, 2½, 3, 3, 3)"

Back

11 (11½, 12, 12½, 13, 13½)"

18"

20½ (22¼, 24¼, 26½, 28½, 30¼)"

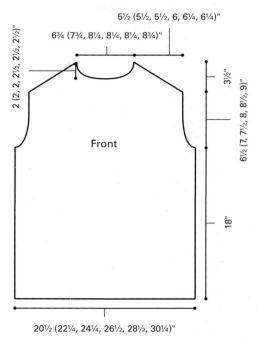

5½ (5½, 5½, 6, 6¼, 6¼)"

6¾ (7¾, 8¼, 8¼, 8¼, 8¾)"

2 (2, 2, 2½, 2½, 2½)"

Front

3½"

6½ (7, 7½, 8, 8½, 9)"

18"

20½ (22¼, 24¼, 26½, 28½, 30¼)"

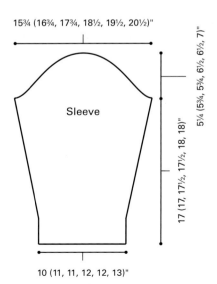

15¾ (16¾, 17¾, 18½, 19½, 20½)"

Sleeve

5¼ (5¾, 5¾, 6½, 6½, 7)"

17 (17, 17½, 17½, 18, 18)"

10 (11, 11, 12, 12, 13)"

# Color Block Jersey

This cotton jersey is perfect for a Saturday afternoon sail and just the right weight for a weekend of apple picking. While the front and back are simple squares, the fun comes into play with the sleeves and saddles, which split, extend forward in the front and back, and meet up under the collar. Feel free to reverse the color combo, putting the darker color in the body and the off-white on the sleeves.

**Skill Level** ▶ Easy

┌─ **MAKE IT MORE FEMININE**

You can add elbow patches if you're making this sweater for a woman. Knit up a 4" × 6" (10cm × 15cm) rectangle in stockinette stitch using the body color. Sew it onto the elbows using a whipstitch so the stitches are visible around the edges.

**Finished Measurements**

| Woman's Size | Man's Size | Bust/Chest | Length |
|---|---|---|---|
| S | XS | 36" (91cm) | 24" (61cm) |
| M | S | 40" (101.5cm) | 25" (63.5cm) |
| L | M | 44" (112cm) | 26½" (67.5cm) |
| XL | L | 48" (122cm) | 27½" (70cm) |
| XXL | XL | 52" (132cm) | 28½" (72cm) |
| XXXL | XXL | 56" (142cm) | 29¾" (75.5cm) |

If only one number is used, it applies to all sizes.
Pictured in size Woman's S in Green and Man's M in Blue

## Materials
- Cascade Yarn Luna (100% cotton, each approximately 1¾ oz [50g] and 82 yd (75m), 9 (10, 10, 11, 12, 13) skeins in color Off White #702 (A), and 5 (5, 6, 6, 6, 7) skeins in color 715 Blue (B) or 748 Green (B), (4) medium
- One pair size U.S. 7 (4.5mm) knitting needles, or size needed to obtain gauge
- Size U.S. 7 (4.5mm) 16" (40cm) circular needle
- Stitch markers
- 4 stitch holders
- Blunt-tip yarn needle

## Gauge
18½ stitches and 26 rows = 4" (10cm) in stockinette stitch
To save time, take time to check gauge.

## Stitch Pattern
**Cuff Rib Pattern** *(multiple of 4 stitches + 2)*
ROW 1 (WS): P2, *k2, p2; repeat from * to end.
ROW 2: K2, *p2, k2; repeat from * to end.
Repeat Row 1 and 2 for the pattern.

**Neck Rib Pattern** *(multiple of 4 stitches)*
ROUND 1 (RS): *K2, p2; repeat from * to end.
Repeat Round 1 for the pattern.

then every 6 rows 7 (5, 3, 2, 3, 0) times, working increases 1 stitch in from the edges (see "A Note About Increasing on Sleeves," p. 18)—88 (92, 100, 106, 110, 116) stitches.

Work even until the piece measures 20 (20½, 21, 21½, 22, 22½)" (51 [52, 53.5, 54.5, 56, 57] cm) from the cast-on edge, ending with a wrong-side row.

### SHAPE SADDLE

Bind off 30 (32, 35, 37, 39, 41) stitches at the beginning of the next 2 rows—28 (28, 30, 32, 32, 34) stitches remain.

Work even until the piece measures 5¼ (5¾, 6½, 7¼, 8¼, 9)" (13.5 [14.5, 16.5, 18.5, 21, 23]cm) from the beginning of the saddle, ending with a right-side row.

### SHAPE RIGHT BACK NECK

NEXT ROW (WS): Purl 14 (14, 15, 16, 16, 17), place the remaining 14 (14, 15, 16, 16, 17) stitches on a holder for the front neck, then turn.

DECREASE ROW (RS): K2tog, knit to the end—13 (13, 14, 15, 15, 16) stitches remain.

Work one wrong-side row then repeat the decrease row—12 (12, 13, 14, 14, 15) stitches remain.

Work even until the piece measures 9 (10, 11, 12, 13, 14)" (23 [25.5, 28, 30.5, 33, 35.5]cm) from the beginning of the saddle. Place the remaining stitches on a holder.

### SHAPE RIGHT FRONT NECK

Slip the 14 (14, 15, 16, 16, 17) right front neck stitches from the holder onto the needle, ready to

## Back

With A and the straight needles, cast on 82 (90, 98, 106, 114, 122) stitches.

Work in the cuff rib pattern until the piece measures 2½" (6.5cm) from the cast-on edge, ending with a right-side row.

NEXT ROW (WS): Work in the cuff rib pattern and increase 1 (2, 4, 5, 6, 8) stitch(es) evenly spaced across the row—83 (92, 102, 111, 120, 130) stitches.

Change to stockinette stitch and work even until the piece measures 14½ (15, 15½, 16, 16½, 17)" (37 [38, 39.5, 40.5, 42, 43] cm) from the cast-on edge. Place a marker at each side for the bottom of the armholes. Continue to work even until the piece measures 21 (22, 23, 24, 25, 26)"

(53.5 [56, 58.5, 61, 63.5, 66]cm) from the cast-on edge. Bind off all stitches.

## Front

Work the same as for the Back.

## Right Sleeve

With B and the straight needles, cast on 42 (42, 46, 46, 50, 50) stitches.

Work in the cuff rib pattern until the piece measures 2½" (6.5cm) from the cast-on edge.

Change to stockinette stitch and work 4 rows even, ending with a wrong-side row.

Increase 1 stitch at each end of the next row, then every 2 rows 2 (3, 5, 7, 7, 8) times, every 4 rows 13 (16, 18, 20, 19, 24) times, work a right-side row. Join the yarn and knit 1 row.

Bind off 2 stitches at the beginning of every wrong-side row 2 (2, 2, 2, 2, 3) times—10 (10, 11, 12, 12, 11) stitches remain.

**DECREASE ROW (RS):** Knit to the last 2 stitches, k2tog—9 (9, 10, 11, 11, 10) stitches remain.

Repeat the decrease row 4 (4, 5, 6, 6, 5) times—5 stitches remain for all sizes.

Work even until the piece measures the same as the back neck and saddle. Place the remaining stitches on a holder.

## Left Sleeve

Work same as for Right Sleeve until the saddle measures 5¼ (5¾, 6½, 7¼, 8¼, 9)" (13.5 [14.5,

16.5, 18.5, 21, 23]cm) from the beginning of the saddle, ending with a wrong-side row.

### SHAPE LEFT BACK NECK
**NEXT ROW (RS):** Knit 12 (12, 13, 14, 14, 15) stitches, k2tog—13 (13, 14, 15, 15, 16) stitches. Place the remaining stitches on a holder for the front neck.

**NEXT ROW (WS):** Purl.

**DECREASE ROW (RS):** Knit to the last 2 stitches, k2tog—12 (12, 13, 14, 14, 15) stitches remain.

Work even until the piece measures 9 (10, 11, 12, 13, 14)" (23 [25.5, 28, 30.5, 33, 35.5]cm) from the beginning of the saddle. Place the remaining stitches on a holder.

### SHAPE LEFT FRONT NECK
Slip the 14 (14, 15, 16, 16, 17) left front neck stitches from the holder onto the needle. Join the yarn to begin with a right-side row.

Bind off 2 stitches at the beginning of every right-side row 2 (2, 2, 2, 2, 3) times—10 (10, 11, 12, 12, 11) stitches remain.

**NEXT ROW (WS):** Purl.

**DECREASE ROW (RS):** K2tog, knit to the end—9 (9, 10, 11, 11, 10) stitches.

Repeat the decrease row 4 (4, 5, 6, 6, 5) times—5 stitches remain for all sizes.

Work even until the piece measures the same as the back neck and saddle. Place the remaining stitches on a holder.

## Finishing

Weave in the ends. Block all the pieces to the finished measurements.

Graft the left and right saddles together using Kitchener stitch.

Sew the Sleeves to the Back and Front between markers, and saddles to the top edges of the Back and Front.

Sew the side and sleeve seams.

## Neckband

With B and the right side facing, use the circular needle to pick up and knit 96 (104, 108, 112, 112, 116) stitches evenly around neck opening. Place a marker for the beginning of the round, and join.

Work in the neck rib pattern for ¾" (2cm). Bind off all stitches in pattern.

## COLOR BLOCK JERSEY **SCHEMATIC**

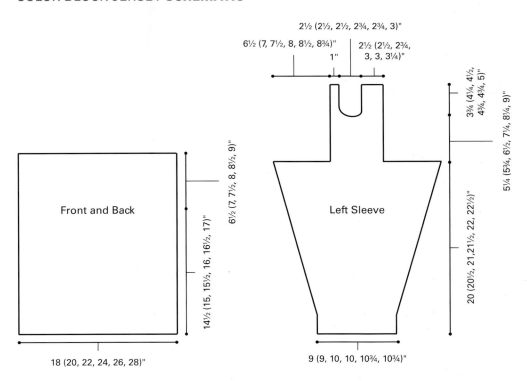

Front and Back

18 (20, 22, 24, 26, 28)"

14½ (15, 15½, 16, 16½, 17)"

6½ (7, 7½, 8, 8½, 9)"

Left Sleeve

9 (9, 10, 10, 10¾, 10¾)"

20 (20½, 21,21½, 22, 22½)"

5¼ (5¾, 6½, 7¼, 8¼, 9)"

3¾ (4¼, 4½, 4¾, 4¾, 5)"

2½ (2½, 2½, 2¾, 2¾, 3)"

6½ (7, 7½, 8, 8½, 8¾)"

1"

2½ (2½, 2¾, 3, 3, 3¼)"

# Camel Cabled Cardigan

Baby camel is a dream to work with. It's so soft on your hands, you won't mind knitting the extra length—even with the cables. Less ribbing and an overall shorter silhouette turns this long cardigan into the perfect man's jacket.

**Skill Level** ▸ Intermediate

## Finished Measurements

| Woman's Size | Man's Size | Bust/Chest | Length |
|---|---|---|---|
| S | XS | 38" (96.5cm) | 30¾" (78cm) |
| M | S | 42" (106.5cm) | 30¾" (78cm) |
| L | M | 46" (117cm) | 30¾" (78cm) |
| XL | L | 50" (127cm) | 30¾" (78cm) |
| XXL | XL | 54" (137cm) | 30¾" (78cm) |

If only one number is used, it applies to all sizes.

## Materials
- Handknitting.com Pure Baby Camel (100% baby camel, each approximately 1¾ oz [50g], 87 yards [79m]; 16 (18, 19, 21, 22) skeins color Natural Brown **(4)** medium
- One pair size U.S. 6 (4mm) needles, or size needed to obtain gauge
- Size U.S. 6 (4mm) 16" (40cm) circular needle
- Cable needle
- Stitch holders
- Blunt-tip yarn needle
- 17 buttons, ½" (13mm) wide

## Gauge
20 stitches and 28 rows = 4" (10cm) in stockinette stitch
To save time, take time to check gauge.

## Stitch Pattern
Cable Panel *(panel of 11 stitches)*
ROW 1 (RS): Slip the next 2 stitches to the cable needle and hold in front, k2 from the left needle, k2 from the cable needle, k3, slip the next 2 stitches to the cable needle and hold in the back, k2 from the left needle, k2 from the cable needle.
ROWS 2 AND 4: Purl.
ROW 3: Knit.
Repeat Rows 1–4 for the pattern.

# Back

With the straight needles, cast on 100 (114, 121, 135, 142) stitches.

**ROW 1 (RS):** K3, *p3, k4; repeat from * to the last 6 stitches, p3, k3.

**ROW 2:** P3, *k3, p4; repeat from * to the last 6 sts, k3, p3.

Repeat Rows 1 and 2 until the piece measures 6" (15cm) from the cast-on edge, ending with a right-side row.

▶ **Sizes 42(50)" (106.5 [127]cm) only:**
**NEXT ROW (WS):** Work in the established pattern and decrease 2 (3) stitches evenly spaced across the row—112 (132) stitches.

▶ **Sizes 38 (46, 54)" (96.5 [117, 137]cm) only:**
**NEXT ROW (WS):** Work in the established pattern and increase 2 (1, 0) stitch(es) evenly spaced across the row—102 (122, 142) stitches.

▶ **All sizes:**
**NEXT ROW (RS):** K27 (31, 35, 39, 43), work Row 1 of the Cable

Panel over the next 11 stitches, k26 (28, 30, 32, 34), work Row 1 of the Cable Panel over the next 11 stitches, k27 (31, 35, 39, 43).

**NEXT ROW:** P27 (31, 35, 39, 43), work Row 2 of the Cable Panel over the next 11 stitches, p26 (28, 30, 32, 34), work Row 2 of the Cable Panel over the next 11 stitches, p27 (31, 35, 39, 43).

Continue working as established until the piece measures 20 (19½, 19, 18½, 18)" (51 [49.5, 48.5, 47, 45.5]cm) from the cast-on edge, ending with a wrong-side row.

## SHAPE ARMHOLES

Bind off 0 (3, 6, 8, 10) stitches at the beginning of the next 0 (2, 2, 2, 2) rows, then 2 stitches at the beginning of the next 0 (2, 2, 4, 4) rows—102 (102, 106, 108, 114) stitches remain.

**DECREASE ROW (RS):** K1, k2tog, work in established pattern to the last 3 stitches, ssk, k1—100 (100, 104, 106, 112) stitches remain.

Repeat the decrease row every RS row 11 (9, 9, 9, 11) more times—78 (82, 86, 88, 90) stitches remain.

Work even until the armhole measures 9½ (10, 10½, 11, 11½)" (24 [25.5, 26.5, 28, 29]cm), ending with a wrong-side row.

## SHAPE SHOULDERS AND NECK

Bind off 4 stitches at the beginning of the next 2 (0, 0, 0, 0) rows, then 5 stitches at the beginning of the following 2 (4, 4, 4, 4) rows—60 (62, 66, 68, 70) stitches remain.

**NEXT ROW (RS):** Bind off 5 (5, 5, 5, 5) stitches, k14 (14, 15, 15, 15), bind off the center 22 (24, 26, 28, 30) stitches for the neck, and work to end. Work each side separately.

## LEFT SHOULDER

Bind off 5 (5, 5, 5, 5) stitches at the beginning of the next wrong-side row, then 4 (4, 5, 5, 5) stitches at the beginning of the following wrong-side row to continue shaping the shoulder. *At the same time,* bind off 3 stitches at the beginning of the next right-side row, then 2 stitches at the beginning of the following right-side row to shape the neck.

Bind off remaining stitches.

## RIGHT SHOULDER

With the wrong side facing, attach the yarn to begin with a wrong-side row.

Bind off 3 stitches at the beginning of the next wrong-side row, then 2 stitches at the beginning of the following wrong-side row to shape the neck. *At the same time,* bind off 5 (5, 5, 5, 5) stitches at the beginning of the next right-side row, then 4 (4, 5, 5, 5) stitches at the beginning of the following right-side row to continue shaping the shoulder.

## WHAT SIDE DO THE BUTTONHOLES GO ON?

Traditionally buttonholes go on the left for a man and on the right side for a woman. While some women don't mind them being on the other side, most men only want them on the left.

# Right Front

With the straight needles, cast on 55 (62, 62, 69, 76) stitches.

**ROW 1 (RS):** (K1, p1) 5 times, *k4, p3; repeat from * to the last 3 stitches, k3.

**ROW 2:** P3, *k3, p4; repeat from * to the last 10 stitches, (k1, p1) 5 times.

Repeat Rows 1 and 2 until the piece measures about 6" (15cm) from the cast-on edge, ending with a right-side row.

▶ **Sizes 46 (50)" (117 [127]cm) only:**
NEXT ROW (WS): Work in the established pattern and increase 3 (1) stitch(es) evenly spaced across the row—65 (70) stitches.

▶ **Sizes 38 (42, 54)" (96.5 [106.5, 137]cm) only:**
NEXT ROW (WS): Work in the established pattern and decrease 0 (2, 1) stitch(es) evenly spaced across the row—55 (60, 75) stitches.

▶ **All sizes**
NEXT ROW (RS): (K1, p1) 5 times, k7 (8, 9, 10, 11), work Row 1 of the Cable Panel over the next 11 stitches, k27 (31, 35, 39, 43).

NEXT ROW (WS): P27 (31, 35, 39, 43), work Row 2 of the Cable Panel over the next 11 stitches, p7 (8, 9, 10, 11), (k1, p1) 5 times.

Continue working as established until the piece measures 20 (19½, 19, 18½, 18)" (51 [49.5, 48.5, 47, 45.5]cm) from the cast-on edge, ending with a right-side row.

## SHAPE ARMHOLE
Bind off at the beginning of wrong-side rows 0 (3, 6, 8, 10)

stitches once, then 2 stitches 0 (1, 1, 2, 2) time(s)—55 (55, 57, 58, 61) stitches remain.

Work 1 (0, 0, 0, 0) row even.

NEXT ROW (RS): (K1, p1) 5 times, work to the last 3 stitches, ssk, k1—54 (54, 56, 57, 60) stitches remain.

Repeat the decrease row every right-side row 11 (9, 9, 9, 11) times more—43 (45, 47, 48, 49) stitches remain.

Work even until the armhole measures 9½ (10, 10½, 11, 11½)" (24 [25.5, 26.5, 28, 29]cm), ending with a right-side row.

## SHAPE SHOULDER
Bind off at the beginning of wrong-side rows 4 stitches 1 (0, 0, 0, 0) time(s), 5 stitches 3 (4, 4, 4, 4) time(s), then 14 (15, 17, 18, 19) stitches once—10 stitches remain.

Continue working rib over the remaining 10 stitches for 2" (5cm). Bind off the remaining stitches in the rib pattern.

# Left Front

With the straight needles, cast on 55 (62, 62, 69, 76) stitches.

**ROW 1 (RS):** K3, *p3, k4; repeat from * to the last 10 stitches, (p1, k1) 5 times.

**ROW 2:** (P1, k1) 5 times, *p4, k3; repeat from * to the last 3 stitches, p3.

**NEXT (BUTTONHOLE) ROW (RS):** Work in the established pattern to the last 6 stitches, slip 1 with the yarn in front, *slip 1 with the yarn in back, pass first slipped stitch over second slipped stitch; repeat from * 2 times more (3 stitches decreased), slip the first stitch on the right needle back to the left needle, turn the work, cable cast-on 4 stitches onto the left needle, turn the work, with the yarn in back slip the first stitch from the left needle to right needle and pass the last cast-on stitch over the slipped stitch, work the remaining 2 stitches in the established pattern.

Continue working even until the piece measures about 6" (15cm) from the cast-on edge, ending with a right-side row, and *at the same time,* work the buttonhole row every 2" (5cm) 16 times more.

▸ **Sizes 46 (50)" (117 [127]cm) only:**
NEXT ROW (WS): Work in the established pattern and increase 3 (1) stitch(es) evenly spaced across the row—65 (70) stitches.

▸ **Sizes 38 (42, 54)" (96.5 [106.5, 137] cm) only:**
NEXT ROW (WS): Work in the established pattern and decrease 0 (2, 1) stitch(es) evenly spaced across the row—55 (60, 75) stitches.

▸ **All sizes**
NEXT ROW (RS): K27 (31, 35, 39, 43), work Row 1 of the Cable Panel over the next 11 stitches, k7 (8, 9, 10, 11), (p1, k1) 5 times.

NEXT ROW (WS): (P1, k1) 5 times, p7 (8, 9, 10, 11), work Row 2 of the Cable Panel over the next 11 stitches, p27 (31, 35, 39, 43).

Continue working as established until the piece measures 20 (19½, 19, 18½, 18)" (51 [49.5, 48.5, 47, 45.5]cm) from the cast-on edge, ending with a wrong-side row.

### SHAPE ARMHOLE
Bind off at the beginning of right-side rows 0 (3, 6, 8, 10) stitches once, then 2 stitches 0 (1, 1, 2, 2) time(s)—55 (55, 57, 58, 61) stitches remain.

Work 1 row even.

NEXT ROW (RS): K1, k2tog, work to the end—54 (54, 56, 57, 60) stitches remain.

Repeat the decrease row every right-side row 11 (9, 9, 9, 11) times more—43 (45, 47, 48, 49) stitches remain.

Work even until the armhole measures 9½ (10, 10½, 11, 11½)" (24, 25.5, 26.5, 28, 29]cm), ending with a wrong-side row.

### SHAPE SHOULDER
Bind off at the beginning of right-side rows 4 stitches 1 (0, 0, 0, 0) time(s), 5 stitches 3 (4, 4, 4, 4) time(s), then 14 (15, 17, 18, 19) stitches once—10 stitches remain.

Continue working rib over the remaining 10 stitches for 2" (5cm). Bind off the remaining stitches in the rib pattern.

## Collar

With the circular needle and the right side facing, begin to the left of the button band, pick up and knit 13 (14, 15, 16, 17) stitches along the right neck, 43 (45, 47, 49, 51) stitches along the back neck, then 13 (14, 15, 16, 17) stitches along the left neck, ending to the right of the buttonhole band—69 (73, 77, 81, 85) stitches.

**ROW 1 (WS):** K1, *p1, k1; repeat from * to the end.

**ROW 2 (RS):** P1, *k1, p1; repeat from * to the end.

Repeat Rows 1 and 2 until the collar measures 2" (5cm), making sure it is the same length as the front bands. Bind off in the rib pattern.

Sew the buttons to the button band, opposite the buttonholes.

## Sleeves (Make 2)

With the straight needles, cast on 50 (54, 54, 58, 58) stitches.

**ROW 1 (RS):** K3, *p2, k2; repeat from * to the last 3 stitches, p3.

Repeat Row 1 until the piece measures 2¾" (7cm) from the cast-on edge, ending with a wrong-side row. Change to stockinette stitch.

**NEXT ROW (RS):** K1, kfb, knit to the last stitch, kfb, k1—52 (56, 56, 60, 60) stitches.

Continue in stockinette stitch and repeat the increase row every 4 rows 15 (9, 13, 15, 23) times, every 6 rows 0 (12, 10, 9, 4) times, then every 8 rows 6 (0, 0, 0, 0) times—94 (98, 102, 108, 114) stitches.

Work even until the piece measures 19 (19½, 20, 20, 20)" (48.5 [49.5, 51, 51, 51]cm) from the cast-on edge, ending with a wrong-side row.

### SHAPE CAP

Bind off 0 (3, 6, 8, 10) stitches at the beginning of the next 0 (2, 2, 2, 2) rows, then 2 stitches at the beginning of the next 0 (2, 2, 4, 4) rows—94 (88, 86, 84, 86) stitches remain.

**NEXT ROW (RS):** K1, k2tog, knit to the last 3 stitches, ssk, k1—92 (86, 84, 82, 84) stitches remain.

Repeat the decrease row every right-side row 11 (9, 9, 9, 11) times more. Bind off the remaining 70 (68, 66, 64, 62) stitches.

## Finishing

Weave in all ends. Block all pieces to the finished measurements.

Sew the shoulder seams, making sure to line up the cables. Sew in the sleeves. Sew the side and sleeve seams.

> ## MAKE IT MORE MASCULINE
>
> ▶ Decrease the body ribbing to 2" (5cm) in all sizes.
>
> ▶ Begin armhole shaping when the pieces measure 14 (14½, 15, 15½, 16)" (35.5 [37, 38, 39.5, 40]cm) from the cast-on edge.
>
> ▶ Decrease the number of buttons by repeating the buttonhole row every 3 inches.

LINE AND DRAPE

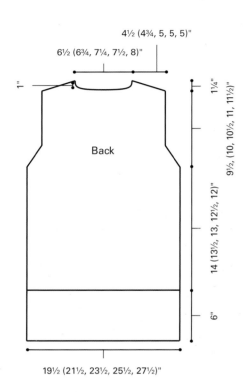

4½ (4¾, 5, 5, 5)"

6½ (6¾, 7¼, 7½, 8)"

1"

Back

1¼"

9½, (10, 10½, 11, 11½)"

14 (13½, 13, 12½, 12)"

6"

19½ (21½, 23½, 25½, 27½)"

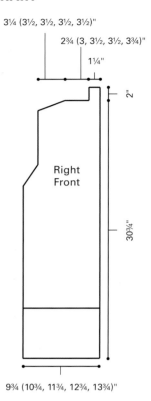

3¼ (3½, 3½, 3½, 3½)"

2¾ (3, 3½, 3½, 3¾)"

1¼"

2"

Right Front

30¾"

9¾ (10¾, 11¾, 12¾, 13¾)"

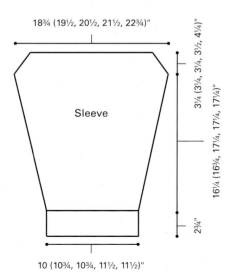

18¾ (19½, 20½, 21½, 22¾)"

3¼ (3¼, 3¼, 3½, 4¼)"

Sleeve

16¼ (16¾, 17¼, 17¼, 17¼)"

2¾"

10 (10¾, 10¾, 11½, 11½)"

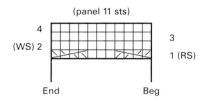

**CABLE PANEL**

(panel 11 sts)

4

(WS) 2

3

1 (RS)

End                    Beg

**STITCH KEY**

☐ = Knit on RS; purl on WS

⟋⟋⟍⟍ = Slip 2 sts to cable needle and hold in front, k2 from left needle, k2 from cable needle

⟍⟍⟋⟋ = Slip 2 sts to cable needle and hold in back, k2 from left needle, k2 from cable needle

# THE **CURSE**

It's a widely held belief that if you knit a sweater for the man you're dating, he'll leave you. Some call it superstition while others say it's absolutely true. It's clearly happened enough that the sweater curse has its own page on Wikipedia and Ravelry.com has one group entirely dedicated to it.

I don't believe in curses, but I do believe that a lot of broken-hearted knitters had horrible experiences knitting for their significant others. But in almost all cases those sweaters didn't cause the boyfriends (or girlfriends) to bolt. The sweaters were the catalysts that pushed these relationships to places they would have ended up anyway.

Many men are afraid of commitment. There are two ways to know if your man is one of them. Option one: Start a discussion about taking your relationship to the next level. For a man who's afraid, that's often his signal to head out the door. If that's too direct, go for option two: Don't bring it up at all. Instead, knit him a lovely Fair Isle sweater. The sweater represents your commitment, in money and countless hours of knitting, but most guys don't know what goes into it. Who among us hasn't let nonknitters know just how much effort a sweater involves, as we seek their gratitude, sympathy, and probably a host of other responses? That's enough to scare off any man who feels he's been dragged into a commitment he hasn't agreed to, even if it only involves yarn.

There could even be a semiscientific excuse for why a man leaves when he gets a hand-knit sweater. Let's say you have a wonderful guy and a happy relationship. He'll do anything to see you smile, including wearing that warm, bulky Fair Isle sweater you made for him. Maybe he even really loves it. What a guy. He puts on the sweater and starts to sweat—a pheromone-rich sweat that radiates out through that gorgeous hand-knit sweater. He now attracts other women like bees to a flower. The next thing you know, he's been uprooted and replanted in another garden.

A sweater can't save a bad relationship. Sometimes we give elaborate gifts to show how much we care about someone and how badly we want them to stay in our lives, even if we know things are not going well. Certainly a hand-knit sweater is a better, if not more affordable, choice than a new car and less messy than a puppy. But we could probably all have stronger relationships if we spent more time talking to our partners instead of giving them gifts.

I've heard that "the curse" is broken when you marry your boyfriend, that knitting for a husband is safe. But even then, proceed with caution. My friend Mary knit a cashmere Aran pullover for her husband—who never wears sweaters and certainly never asked her to make one. Two months later he gave it to a local thrift store; Mary didn't talk to him for weeks. True, he didn't leave over a sweater, but she almost did.

Just remember, if your relationship ends over a sweater, it's not the sweater. And the best thing you can do in that situation is keep that sweater and wear it yourself. He doesn't deserve you, and he doesn't deserve the sweater, either.

# 2.

# TEXTURE

The following projects are all about the look and feel of the knit fabric. Slipping stitches, gathering those slipped stitches, and knitting into rows below create woven and three-dimensional knits that are both understated and sophisticated.

# SHAKER RIB STITCH,
## OR KNITTING ONE BELOW

This stitch is sometimes referred to as Brioche, English Rib, or Fisherman Rib. It's not difficult because you are going to simply knit every wrong-side row. Right-side rows are a combination of purling and knitting—but the knits on the right-side row are where things get interesting. Instead of knitting into the next stitch waiting for you on your left-hand needle, you are going to knit into the stitch one row directly below. Take a close look and you'll see that the next stitch on your left-hand needle is coming up out of the loop below it. The sides of *that* loop form a V—that V is the stitch below that stitch. To knit into the stitch below, insert your needle, front to back, into the space inside that V. Wrap or grab your working yarn, and pull it back through. When you drop the old stitch from your left-hand needle, you're actually dropping 2 stitches—one above the other.

## SLIPPED STITCHES

To see how slipped stitches create texture, examine the anatomy of the slipped stitch. Slipping the stitch from the left needle to the right without knitting or purling it means the working yarn will cross over the slipped stitch. Slip the stitch with the working yarn in the front (a) and it will be visible on the front side of the garment. Slip the stitch with the working yarn in the back (b) and it will be

visible on the back side of the garment. Either way, the yarn is visible as a small horizontal line.

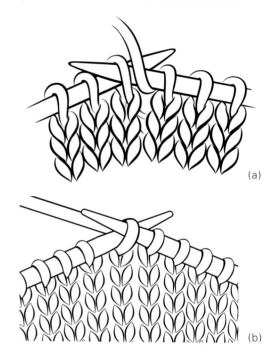

(a)

(b)

## WOVEN STITCHES—
## LINEN AND TWEED

Linen stitch (opposite, above) is created by knitting one row and purling the next, just like in stockinette. But in both rows, every other stitch is slipped and all of those horizontal lines, created by the slipped stitches, begin to look like the weft yarn in weaving, or threads that are woven from left to right over and under the horizontal warp threads on a loom. The knit fabric looks like woven linen. But there is a trick to getting it right. Always knit or purl the stitches that were slipped in the previous row and slip the stitches that were worked in the previous row. This might mean that the first or last stitch in a row is slipped. That's okay. If the knit piece starts to look like ribs instead of woven fabric, you've slipped the same stitch twice in a row.

Tweed stitch (below, bottom) is just like linen stitch, but you do not slip any stitches on the back, or purl side, rows, just on the front, or knit side, rows. The trick here is to make sure that stitches worked on the previous front side rows are slipped and stitches slipped on previous front side rows are worked.

For a more feminine variation of tweed stitch, purl all stitches on both sides but slip every other stitch on the front side. The same rules apply—purl the slipped stitches from the previous front side row and slip the purled stitches from the previous front side row.

*Linen stitch*

*Tweed stitch*

# GATHERED SLIPPED STITCHES

Slipping more than one stitch at a time creates longer horizontal lines, for more dramatic and complex three-dimensional patterns. To give these slipped

stitches even more life, they can be gathered, as in the Honeycomb Pullover (see page 75). To create this effect, slip three stitches in a row on the right side, forming a longer horizontal line visible across the front. On the following right-side row, slip the same three stitches, creating a pair of parallel horizontal lines (a). On the third right-side row, stop at the three slipped stitches. Knit the first of the three normally. To knit the second one, pass the right-hand needle under and behind that pair of parallel lines, then reach up and knit the next stitch (b), pulling the new stitch back under those lines before dropping the old stitch off the left-hand needle. The two parallel lines will be caught inside the new stitch and pulled upward, creating a three-dimensional effect. Knit the third stitch in the normal manner. By repeating this three-stitch element in strategic areas, the honeycomb look is achieved.

(a)

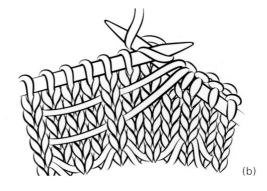

(b)

# **Shaker** Cardigan

This Shaker rib stitch is a relative of brioche knitting. But unlike traditional brioche, which is worked on both sides, this pattern is only slipped on the right side, creating a warm, comforting cardigan that isn't too bulky or heavy. The contrasting rib on the inside adds visual interest when the sweater is worn open.

**Skill Level** ▶ Easy

**Finished Measurements**

| Woman's Size | Man's Size | Bust/Chest | Length |
|---|---|---|---|
| S | XS | 35" (89cm) | 27½" (70cm) |
| M | S | 39" (99cm) | 28" (71cm) |
| L | M | 43" (109cm) | 28½" (72cm) |
| XL | L | 47" (119.5cm) | 29" (74cm) |
| XXL | XL | 51" (129.5cm) | 29½" (75cm) |
| XXXL | XXL | 55" (139.5cm) | 30" (76cm) |

If only one number is used, it applies to all sizes.

**Materials**
- Blue Sky Alpacas Worsted Hand Dyes (50% royal alpaca, 50% merino, each approximately 3½ oz [100g] and 100 yards [91m]; 12 (13, 14, 16, 17, 18) skeins in color 2016 Chocolate, (**4**) medium
- Size U.S. 7 (4.5mm) 29" (74cm) circular needle, or size needed to obtain gauge
- Size U.S. 8 (5mm) 40" (101.5cm) circular needle
- Size U.S. 9 (5.5mm) 29" (74cm) circular needle
- Blunt-tip yarn needle
- 5 buttons, 1" (25mm) wide

**Gauge**

16 sts and 32 rows = 4" (10cm) in Shaker rib pattern with size U.S 7 (4.5mm) needles
To save time, take time to check gauge.

**Stitch Patterns**

Shaker Rib *(multiple of 2 stitches)*
ROW 1 (RS): K1, *k1b, p1; repeat from * to the last stitch, k1.
ROW 2 (WS): Knit.
Repeat Rows 1 and 2 for the pattern
K1b = knit into the stitch in the row below (see page 52)

K1, P1 Rib *(multiple of 2 stitches)*
ROW 1 (RS): K1, *k1, p1; repeat from * to the last stitch, k1.
Repeat Row 1 for the pattern.

Change to size U.S. 7 (4.5mm) needles. Knit 1 wrong-side row. Work in the Shaker rib pattern until the piece measures 13" (33cm) from the cast-on edge, ending with a wrong-side row.

### SHAPE NECK

Decrease 1 stitch at the beginning of the next right-side row, then every 4 rows 0 (0, 0, 0, 3, 10) times, every 6 rows 0 (0, 7, 8, 6, 0) times, then every 8 rows 5 (6, 0, 0, 0, 0) times—28 (31, 34, 37, 40, 43) stitches remain. Continue even until the piece measures 19" (48.5cm) from the cast-on edge, ending with a right-side row.

### SHAPE ARMHOLE

Bind off 3 (4, 5, 6, 7, 8) stitches at the beginning of the next row— 25 (27, 29, 31, 33, 35) stitches remain. Work 8 rows even.

**NEXT ROW (RS):** Work in the Shaker rib pattern to the last 4 stitches, ssk, p1, k1—24 (26, 28, 30, 32, 34) stitches remain.

Work 1 row even.

Repeat the last 2 rows 21 (23, 25, 27, 29, 31) times more—3 stitches remain.

Work 8 rows even. Bind off all stitches.

## Left Front

With size U.S. 9 (5.5mm) needles, cast on 34 (38, 42, 46, 50, 54) stitches.

Work in the k1, p1 rib pattern for 3" (7.5cm), ending with a right-side row.

Change to size U.S. 7 (4.5mm) needles. Knit 1 wrong-side row.

## Back

With size U.S. 9 (5.5mm) needle, cast on 72 (80, 88, 96, 104, 112) stitches.

Work in the k1, p1 rib pattern for 3" (7.5cm), ending with a right-side row.

Change to size U.S. 7 (4.5mm) needle. Knit 1 wrong-side row. Work in the Shaker rib pattern until the piece measures 19" (48.5cm) from the cast-on edge, ending with a wrong-side row.

### SHAPE ARMHOLES

Bind off 3 (4, 5, 6, 7, 8) stitches at the beginning of the next 2 rows—66 (72, 78, 84, 90, 96) stitches remain.

Work 8 rows even.

**NEXT ROW (RS):** K1, k2tog, work in the Shaker rib pattern to the last 4 stitches, ssk, p1, k1—64 (70, 76, 82, 88, 94) stitches remain.

Work 1 row even.

Repeat the last 2 rows 21 (23, 25, 27, 29, 31) times more—22 (24, 26, 28, 30, 32) stitches remain.

Work 8 rows even. Bind off all stitches.

## Right Front

With size U.S. 9 (5.5mm) needles, cast on 34 (38, 42, 46, 50, 54) stitches.

Work in the k1, p1 rib pattern for 3" (7.5cm), ending with a right-side row.

Work in the Shaker rib pattern until the piece measures 13" (33cm) from the cast-on edge, ending with a right-side row.

**SHAPE NECK**

Decrease 1 stitch at the beginning of the next wrong-side row, then every 4 rows 0 (0, 0, 0, 3, 10) times, then every 6 rows 0 (0, 7, 8, 6, 0) times, then every 8 rows 5 (6, 0, 0, 0, 0) times—28 (31, 34, 37, 40, 43) stitches remain. Continue even until the piece measures 19" (48.5cm) from the cast-on edge, ending with a wrong-side row.

**SHAPE ARMHOLE**

Bind off 3 (4, 5, 6, 7, 8) stitches at the beginning of the next row—25 (27, 29, 31, 33, 35) stitches remain.

Work 7 rows even.

**NEXT ROW (RS):** K1, k2tog, work in the Shaker rib pattern to the end—24 (26, 28, 30, 32, 34) stitches remain.

Work 1 row even.

Repeat the last 2 rows 21 (23, 25, 27, 29, 31) times more—3 stitches remain.

Work 8 rows even. Bind off all stitches.

## Sleeves (Make 2)

With size U.S. 9 (5.5mm) needle, cast on 30 (32, 34, 36, 38, 40) stitches.

Work in the K1, P1 Rib pattern for 2½" (6.5cm), ending with a right-side row.

Change to size U.S. 7 (4.5mm) needles. Knit 1 wrong-side row.

Work in the Shaker Rib pattern and increase 1 stitch at each end of the first row, then every 6 rows 0 (0, 2, 9, 16, 23) times, then every 8 rows 3 (10, 15, 10, 5, 0) times, then every 10 rows 10 (5, 0, 0, 0, 0) times—58 (64, 70, 76, 82, 88) stitches. Work the new stitches into the pattern.

Work even until the piece measures 19¾ (20, 20¼, 20½, 20¾, 21)" (50 [51, 51.5. 52, 52.5, 53.5] cm) from the cast-on edge, ending with a wrong-side row.

**SHAPE CAP**

Bind off 3 (4, 5, 6, 7. 8) stitches at the beginning of the next 2 rows—52 (56, 60, 64, 68, 72) stitches remain.

Work 8 rows even.

**NEXT ROW (RS):** K1, k2tog, work in the Shaker rib pattern to the last 4 stitches, ssk, p1, k1—50 (54, 58, 62, 66, 70) stitches remain.

Work 1 row even.

Repeat the last 2 rows 21 (23, 25, 27, 29, 31) times more— 8 stitches remain.

Work 8 rows even. Bind off all stitches.

## Finishing

Weave in all ends. Sew in the sleeves. Sew the side and sleeve seams.

## Neckband

With the size U.S. 8 (5mm) needle and the right side facing, start at the bottom edge of the right front and pick up and knit 112 (114, 117, 119, 122, 124) stitches along the

Right Front edge, 6 stitches along the top of the right Sleeve, 27 (29, 31, 33, 35, 37) stitches along the Back neck edge, 6 along the top of the left Sleeve, and 112 (114, 117. 119, 122, 124) stitches down along the Left Front edge—263 (269, 277, 283, 291, 297) stitches. Make sure there are 56 stitches along the unshaped edge of both Front edges.

ROW 1 (WS): P1, *k1, p1; repeat from * to the end.

ROW 2: K1, *p1, k1; repeat from * to the end.

Work 1 row more in the established pattern.

NEXT (BUTTONHOLE) ROW (RS): Work to the last 56 stitches, *bind off 2 stitches for the buttonhole, work 11 stitches; repeat from * 3 times more, bind off 2 stitches, work the remaining 2 stitches.

NEXT ROW (WS): Work in the rib pattern and cast on 2 stitches over each buttonhole gap.

Work 1 row even in the rib pattern. Bind off all stitches in the rib pattern.

## MAKE IT MORE FEMININE

- ▸ Use larger buttons
- ▸ Increase bottom ribbing to 4" (10cm) in all sizes
- ▸ Increase body length by 2" (5cm) in all sizes before beginning raglan armhole shaping

## SHAKER CARDIGAN **SCHEMATIC AND CHART**

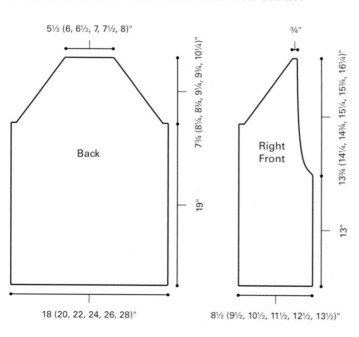

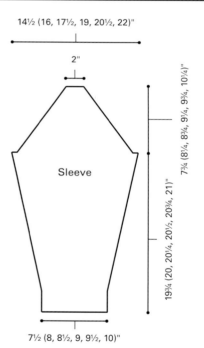

**SHAKER RIB**

(mult 2 sts)

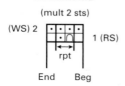

**STITCH KEY**

☐ = Knit on RS, purl on WS

· = Purl on RS, knit on WS

∩ = K1b = knit 1 in the row below

# Linen Scarf or Wrap

Both versions of this pattern use the same stitch, but the overall effect is quite different. The scarf (opposite, right) is knit the short way, making the look more masculine and the design begins to take shape quickly. The wrap (opposite, left) requires knitting rows the long way, and you won't begin to see the pattern emerge until you've completed an inch or so. Either way, don't be tempted to use smaller needles than called for. Larger needles are necessary to keep this stitch from becoming too tight.

**Skill Level** ▸ Easy

**Finished Measurements**

| Size | Width | Length |
|------|-------|--------|
| Narrow | 9¾" (25cm) | 76" (193cm) |
| Wide | 11" (28cm) | 62¼" (158cm) |

Instructions are for the narrower size, with changes for the wider size noted in parentheses as necessary; if only one number is used, it applies to both sizes.

Narrow scarf pictured in 3112 Moss; wide wrap pictured in 3104 Prairie

**Materials**
- Manos del Uruguay Silk Blend (30% silk, 70% merino wool, each approximately 1¾ oz [50g] and 150 yd [135m]), 6 (5) skeins in color 3122 Moss (A) or 3104 Prairie (B), ⓛ light
- Size U.S. 8 (5mm) 40" (100cm) circular needle, or size needed to obtain gauge
- Blunt-tip yarn needle

**Gauge**
29 stitches and 52 rows = 4" (10cm) in linen stitch
To save time, take time to check gauge.

**Stitch Pattern**
Linen Stitch (*odd number of stitches*)
ROW 1 (RS): K1, *slip st purlwise with yarn in front, k1; repeat from * to end.
ROW 2: K1, p1, *slip st purlwise with yarn in back, p1; repeat from * to last st, k1.
Repeat Rows 1 and 2 for the pattern.

**Note**
The narrower scarf is worked from end to end, while the wider wrap is knit from side to side.

## MAKE IT MORE NEUTRAL

Men are often willing to wear a scarf with more color than they might wear otherwise. Try 3303 Spumoni (top), 3105 Lava (middle), or 3119 Adobe (bottom). Continue to work the short way for a man's scarf and the long way for a more feminine look.

## Scarf

With A (B), cast on 71 (451) stitches.

Work even in Linen Stitch until the piece measures 76 (11)" (193 [28]cm) from the cast-on edge, ending with a wrong-side row.

Bind off in pattern.

## Finishing

Weave in all ends. Block piece to the finished measurements.

## LINEN SCARF OR WRAP **CHART**

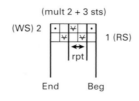

(mult 2 + 3 sts)

(WS) 2

1 (RS)

rpt

End     Beg

### STITCH KEY

□ = K on RS; p on WS

· = K on WS

⅄ = Slip st purlwise with yarn in front on RS rows; slip st purlwise yarn in back on WS rows

# Seed Placket Pullover

With leather buttons and tailored sleeves, this sweater can be worn to all but the most formal of occasions. Although the torso is unshaped, simple vertical stripes of seed stitch act as slimming ribbed accents.

**Skill Level** ▸ Intermediate

## Finished Measurements

| Woman's Size | Man's Size | Bust/Chest | Length |
| --- | --- | --- | --- |
| S | XS | 36" (91cm) | 23½" (59.5cm) |
| M | S | 40" (101.5cm) | 24½" (62cm) |
| L | M | 44" (112cm) | 25½" (65cm) |
| XL | L | 48" (122cm) | 26½" (67.5cm) |
| XXL | XL | 52" (132cm) | 27½" (70cm) |
| XXXL | XXL | 56" (142cm) | 28½" (72cm) |

If only one number is used, it applies to all sizes.
Pictured in size Woman's Medium/Man's Small

## Materials

- Shibui Knits Merino Worsted (100% superwash merino wool, each approximately 3½ oz [100g] and 191 yds [175m]), 7 (7, 8, 9, 9, 10) skeins in color Seaweed, Peacock, or Chinese Red, 4 medium
- One pair size U.S. 6 (4mm) needles, or size needed to obtain gauge
- Size U.S. 6 (4mm) 26" (66cm) circular needle
- Stitch holder
- Blunt-tip yarn needle
- 2 buttons, ¾" (19 mm) wide

## Gauge

20 stitches and 27 rows = 4" (10cm) in stockinette stitch
To save time, take time to check gauge.

## Stitch Patterns

**Body Rib Pattern** *(multiple of 5 stitches)*
ROW 1 (RS): K4, *p2, k3, repeat from * to last stitch, k1.
ROW 2 (WS): P4, *k2, p3, repeat from * to last stitch, p1.
Repeat Rows 1 and 2 for the pattern.

**Sleeve Rib Pattern** *(multiple of 5 stitches + 2)*
ROW 1 (RS): K2, *p2, k3; repeat from * to the end.
ROW 2 (WS): *P3, k2; repeat from * to the last 2 sts, p2.
Repeat Rows 1 and 2 for the pattern.

**Stockinette with Seeded Rib** *(multiple of 12 stitches + 2)*
ROW 1 (RS): *P1, k11, repeat from * to the last 2 stitches, p1, k1.
ROW 2 (WS): *K1, p11, repeat from * to the last 2 stitches, k1, p1.
Repeat Rows 1 and 2 for the pattern.

Seed Stitch *(multiple of 2 stitches)*
ROW 1 (WS): *K1, p1; repeat from *
to the end.
ROW 2 (RS): *P1, k1; repeat from *
to the end.
Repeat Rows 1 and 2 for the pattern.

## Back

With the straight needles, cast on 90 (100, 110, 120, 130, 140) stitches.

Work in body rib pattern until the piece measures about 2½" (6.5cm) from the cast-on edge, ending with a right-side row.

NEXT ROW (WS): Work in the rib pattern and increase 2 stitches evenly spaced across the row—92 (102, 112, 122, 132, 142) stitches.

NEXT ROW (RS): K3 (8, 7, 6, 5, 4), work the stockinette with seeded rib pattern to the last 3 (8, 7, 6, 5, 4) stitches, k3 (8, 7, 6, 5, 4).

NEXT ROW: P3 (8, 7, 6, 5, 4), work the stockinette with seeded rib pattern to the last 3 (8, 7, 6, 5, 4) stitch(es), p3 (8, 7, 6, 5, 4).

Continue to work even until the piece measures 15½ (16, 16½, 17, 17½, 18)" (39.5 [40.5, 42, 43, 44.5, 45.5]cm) from the cast-on edge, ending with a wrong-side row.

### SHAPE ARMHOLES

Bind off 5 (7, 7, 8, 8, 10) stitches at the beginning of the next 2 rows, then 2 stitches at the beginning of the next 0 (0, 2, 2, 4, 6) rows—82 (88, 94, 102, 108, 110) stitches remain.

NEXT ROW (RS): K2, ssk, work in the pattern to the last 4 stitches, k2tog, k2.

Work 1 wrong-side row even.

Repeat the last 2 rows 7 (8, 8, 10, 10, 9) times more—66 (70, 76, 80, 86, 90) stitches remain.

Work even in the pattern until the armhole measures 7½ (8, 8½, 9, 9½, 10)" (19 [20.5, 21.5, 23, 24, 25.5]cm), ending with a wrong-side row.

### SHAPE SHOULDERS

Bind off 9 (10, 11, 11, 12, 13) stitches at the beginning of the next 4 rows. Bind off the remaining 30 (30, 32, 36, 38, 38) stitches for the neck.

## Front

Work the Front same as the Back until the piece measures 14 (14½, 15, 15½, 16, 16½)" (35.5 [37, 38, 39.5, 40.5, 42]cm) from the cast-on edge, ending with a wrong-side row.

### DIVIDE FOR PLACKET

NEXT ROW (RS): Work 31 (36, 40, 43, 47, 52) stitches in the pattern, place the remaining 61 (66, 72, 79, 85, 90) stitches on a holder. Turn and work the left front in the pattern until the piece measures 15½ (16, 16½, 17, 17½, 18)" (39.5 [40.5, 42, 43, 44.5, 45.5]cm) from the cast-on edge, ending with a wrong-side row.

### SHAPE LEFT ARMHOLE

Bind off at the beginning of right-side rows 5 (7, 7, 8, 8, 10) stitches once, then 2 stitches 0 (0, 1, 1, 2, 3) time(s)—26 (29, 31, 33, 35, 36) stitches remain.

Work 1 wrong-side row even.

Work even in the pattern until the armhole measures 7½ (8, 8½, 9,

NEXT ROW (RS): K2, ssk, work in the pattern to the end.

Repeat the last 2 rows 7 (8, 8, 10, 10, 9) times more—18 (20, 22, 22, 24, 26) stitches remain.

Work even in the pattern until the armhole measures 7½ (8, 8½, 9, 9½, 10)" (19 [20.5, 21.5, 23, 24, 25.5]cm), ending with a wrong-side row.

### SHAPE LEFT SHOULDER

Bind off 9 (10, 11, 11, 12, 13) stitches at the beginning of the next 2 right-side rows.

### RIGHT SIDE OF FRONT

With right side facing, place sts from holder back on the straight needle. Join the yarn to begin with a right-side row.

NEXT ROW (RS): Bind off 30 (30, 32, 36, 38, 38) stitches, then work to the end—31 (36, 40, 43, 47, 52) stitches remain. Work even in the pattern until the piece measures 15½ (16, 16½, 17, 17½, 18)" (39.5 [40.5, 42, 43, 44.5, 45.5]cm) from the cast-on edge, ending with a right-side row.

### SHAPE RIGHT ARMHOLE

Bind off at the beginning of wrong-side rows 5 (7, 7, 8, 8, 10) stitches once, then 2 stitches 0 (0, 1, 1, 2, 3) time(s)—26 (29, 31, 33, 35, 36) stitches remain.

Work 1 right-side row even.

NEXT ROW (WS): P2, p2tog, work in the pattern to the end.

Repeat the last 2 rows 7 (8, 8, 10, 10, 9) times more—18 (20, 22, 22, 24, 26) stitches remain.

Work even in the pattern until the armhole measures 7½ (8, 8½, 9,

9½, 10)" (19 [20.5, 21.5, 23, 24, 25.5]cm), ending with a right-side row.

## SHAPE RIGHT SHOULDER

Bind off 9 (10, 11, 11, 12, 13) stitches at the beginning of the next 2 wrong-side rows.

## Sleeves (Make 2)

With the straight needles, cast on 42 (47, 47, 52, 52, 57) stitches.

Work in the sleeve rib pattern until the piece measures about 2½" (6.5cm), ending with a right-side row.

NEXT ROW (WS): Work in the rib pattern and increase 2 (1, 1, 2, 2, 1) stitch(es) evenly spaced across the row—44 (48, 48, 54, 54, 58) stitches.

NEXT ROW (RS): K3 (5, 5, 2, 2, 4), work the stockinette with seeded rib pattern to the last 3 (5, 5, 2, 2, 4) stitches, k3 (5, 5, 2, 2, 4).

NEXT ROW: P3 (5, 5, 2, 2, 4), work the stockinette with seeded rib pattern to the last 3 (5, 5, 2, 2, 4) stitches, p3 (5, 5, 2, 2, 4).

Continue in the stockinette with seeded rib pattern and increase 1 stitch at each side of every 6 rows 0 (0, 0, 0, 7, 12) times, every 8 rows 0 (5, 12, 12, 7, 3) times, then every 10 rows 9 (5, 0, 0, 0, 0) times, working the new stitches in the stockinette with seeded rib pattern—62 (68, 72, 78, 82, 88) stitches.

Continue even until the piece measures 17 (17, 17½, 17½, 18, 18)" (43 [43, 44.5, 44.5, 45.5, 45.5]cm) from the cast-on edge, ending with a wrong-side row.

## SHAPE CAP

Bind off 5 (7, 7, 8, 8, 10) stitches at the beginning of the next 2 rows, then 2 stitches at the beginning of the next 0 (0, 2, 2, 4, 6) rows—52 (54, 54, 58, 58, 56) stitches remain.

DECREASE ROW (RS): K2, ssk, work in the pattern to the last 4 stitches, k2tog, k2.

Work 3 rows even.

Repeat the last 4 rows 7 (7, 6, 6, 6, 6) times more, then repeat the decrease row every right-side row 5 (6, 7, 8, 7, 7) times—26 (26, 26, 28, 30, 28) stitches remain.

Bind off 4 stitches at the beginning of the next 2 rows.

Bind off the remaining 18 (18, 18, 20, 22, 20) stitches.

## Finishing

Weave in all the ends. Block all pieces to the finished measurements.

Sew the shoulder seams.

## Collar

With the circular needle, cast on 1 stitch and leave a tail about 18" (45.5cm) long, with the right side facing, begin at the lower right side of the neck opening and pick up and knit 46 (48, 50, 52, 54, 56) stitches along the right front edge, 30 (30, 32, 36, 38, 38) stitches across the back

## MAKE IT MORE FEMININE

In green with leather buttons, this sweater is gender-neutral. For a more feminine look, try a brighter color like Peacock (left) or Chinese Red (right). Also, leave off the buttons and skip the buttonhole.

neck edge, 46 (48, 50, 52, 54, 56) stitches along the left front edge, cast on 1 stitch—124 (128, 134, 142, 148, 152) stitches.

Work in the seed stitch pattern until the piece measures 4" (10cm), ending with a right-side row.

**BUTTONHOLE ROW (WS):** Work 4 stitches in the pattern, k2tog, yarn over, work 10 stitches in the pattern, k2tog, yarn over, work in the pattern to the end.

**NEXT ROW (RS):** Work in the pattern and knit the yarn overs.

Work 5 rows more in the pattern. Bind off all stitches in the pattern.

Using the long tail from the first cast-on stitch, sew the edges of the placket to the bound-off edge at the bottom of the opening, overlapping the ends with the

buttonholes in front, and using the cast-on stitch at each end as the seam allowance.

Set in the sleeves. Sew the side and sleeve seams.

Sew the top button to the right collar opposite the buttonhole.

The bottom button is decorative. Sew it on the same level as the lower buttonhole, but directly under the first button.

## SEED PLACKET PULLOVER SCHEMATIC

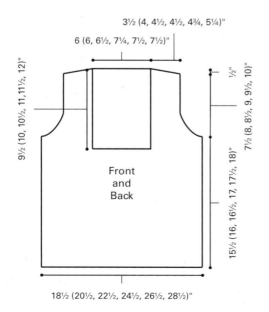

3½ (4, 4½, 4½, 4¾, 5¼)"

6 (6, 6½, 7¼, 7½, 7½)"

9½ (10, 10½, 11, 11½, 12)"

½"

7½ (8, 8½, 9, 9½, 10)"

Front and Back

15½ (16, 16½, 17, 17½, 18)"

18½ (20½, 22½, 24½, 26½, 28½)"

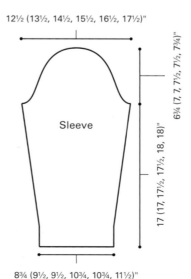

12½ (13½, 14½, 15½, 16½, 17½)"

6¾ (7, 7, 7½, 7½, 7¾)"

Sleeve

17 (17, 17½, 17½, 18, 18)"

8¾ (9½, 9½, 10¾, 10¾, 11½)"

**Textured Argyle** Cardigan

# Textured Argyle Cardigan

Sometimes texture can be added without fancy techniques, just a simple manipulation of knit and purl stitches. In this case, the use of stockinette and reverse stockinette creates an argyle pattern that is a tone-on-tone tour de force. And it's a snap to knit with the body constructed in one piece—no side seams to sew!

**Skill Level** ▶ Easy

**Finished Measurements**

| Woman's Size | Man's Size | Bust/Chest | Length |
|---|---|---|---|
| S | XS | 35½" (90cm) | 25½" (65cm) |
| M | S | 39½" (100.5cm) | 26¼" (66.5cm) |
| L | M | 43½" (110.5cm) | 27" (68.5cm) |
| XL | L | 47½" (120.5cm) | 27¾" (70.5cm) |
| XXL | XL | 51½" (131cm) | 28½" (72cm) |
| XXXL | XXL | 55½" (141cm) | 29¼" (74.5cm) |

If only one number is used, it applies to all sizes.
Pictured in size Woman's Large/Man's Medium

**Materials**
- Kollage Fantastic (100% merino wool, each approximately 1¾ oz [50g] and 93 yd [85m]), 14 (15, 17, 19, 20, 22) skeins color 7518 Dark Shadow, (4) medium
- Size U.S. 7 (4.5mm) 36" (91cm) circular needle, or size needed to obtain gauge
- One pair size U.S. 7 (4.5mm) needles
- Stitch holders
- Blunt-tip yarn needle
- 6 buttons, ¾" (2cm) wide

**Gauge**
20 stitches and 26 rows = 4" (10cm) in stockinette stitch
To save time, take time to check gauge.

**Stitch Patterns**
Banded Rib (multiple of 4 stitches + 1)
ROW 1 (RS): P4, *k1, p3; repeat from * to the last stitch, p1.
ROW 2 (WS): K4, *p1, k3; repeat from * to the last stitch, k1.
Repeat Rows 1 and 2 for the pattern.

K1, P1 Rib (odd number of stitches)
ROW 1 (RS): K1, *p1, k1; repeat from * to the end.
ROW 2 (WS): P1, *k1, p1; repeat from * to the end.
Repeat Rows 1 and 2 for the pattern.

**Note**
A double yarn over is used when making each buttonhole. On the row following the buttonhole, drop the first yarn over of each double yarn over, then work the second yarn over in the rib pattern; the double yarn over creates a larger buttonhole.

## Body

With the circular needle, cast on 173 (193, 213, 233, 253, 273) stitches.

Work in the banded rib pattern until the piece measures 2½" (6.5cm) from the cast-on edge, ending with a right-side row. Bind off knitwise on the next wrong-side row.

With the circular needle, and the wrong side facing, pick up and knit 173 (193, 213, 233, 253, 273) stitches just below the bound-off edge, creating a straight, visible ridge on the right side of the sweater.

NEXT ROW (RS): K14, work Row 1 of chart over the next 23 stitches, k8 (18, 28, 38, 48, 58), work Row 1 of chart over the next 23 stitches, (k7, work Row 1 of chart over the next 23 stitches) twice, k8 (18, 28, 38, 48, 58), work Row 1 of chart over the next 23 stitches, k14.

NEXT ROW: P14, work Row 2 of chart over the next 23 stitches, p8 (18, 28, 38, 48, 58), work Row 2 of chart over the next 23 stitches, (p7, work Row 2 of chart over the next 23 stitches) twice, p8 (18, 28, 38, 48, 58), work Row 2 of chart over the next 23 stitches, p14.

Continue working as established, working stockinette stitch between argyle panels, and repeat Rows 9–24 of the chart until the piece measures 16½ (16¾, 17, 17¼, 17½, 17¾)" (42 [42.5, 43, 44, 44.5, 45]cm) from banded rib cast-on edge, ending with a right-side row.

### DIVIDE FOR ARMHOLES

NEXT ROW (WS): Work across 41 (46, 51, 56, 61, 66) stitches of the left front and slip them to a holder, work the next 91 (101, 111, 121, 131, 141) stitches for the back and slip the remaining 41 (46, 51, 56, 61, 66) stitches to a holder for the right front.

## Back

Continuing in the established pattern, bind off 2 stitches at the beginning of the next 0 (0, 0, 2, 2, 4) rows. Decrease 1 stitch at the beginning of the next 6 (8, 10, 12, 16, 18) rows—85 (93, 101, 105, 111, 115) stitches remain.

Work even until the piece measures 25½ (26¼, 27, 27¾, 28½, 29¼)" (65 [66.5, 68.5, 70.5, 72, 74.5]cm) from the banded rib cast-on edge.

Bind off all stitches.

## Right Front

Return the 41 (46, 51, 56, 61, 66) stitches held for the right front to the straight needles. Join the yarn to begin with a wrong-side row. Continuing in the established pattern, bind off 2 stitches at the beginning of every wrong-side row 0 (0, 0, 1, 1, 2) time(s). Decrease 1 stitch at the armhole edge of every wrong-side row 3 (4, 5, 6, 8, 9) times—38 (42, 46, 48, 51, 53) stitches remain.

### SHAPE NECK

DECREASE ROW (RS): K1, ssk, work in the pattern to the end of the row—37 (41, 45, 47, 50, 52) stitches remain.

Repeat the decrease row every 4 rows 0 (0, 2, 6, 9, 12) times, then every 6 rows 7 (8, 7, 4, 2, 0) times—30 (33, 36, 37, 39, 40) stitches remain.

Work even until the Front measures the same as the Back to the shoulder. Bind off the remaining stitches.

## Left Front

Work the same as for the right front, reversing all shaping.

Note that decrease row will start on a WS as P1, p2tog.

## Sleeves (Make 2)

With the straight needles, cast on 41 (45, 45, 49, 53, 57) stitches.

Work in the banded rib pattern until the piece measures 2½" (6.5cm), ending with a right-side row. Bind off knitwise on the next wrong-side row.

With the straight needles, and the wrong side facing, pick up and knit 41 (45, 45, 49, 53, 57) stitches just below the bound-off edge.

NEXT ROW (RS): Working in stockinette stitch, increase 1 stitch at each side of this row; repeat every 2 rows 0 (0, 0, 1, 1, 2) time(s), every 4 rows 16 (18, 24, 24, 24, 24) times, then every 6 rows 5 (4, 0, 0, 0, 0) times—85 (90, 95, 100, 105, 110) stitches. Continue even until the Sleeve measures 19" (48.5cm) from banded rib cast-on edge, ending with a right-side row.

### SHAPE CAP
Bind off 2 stitches at the beginning of the next 0 (0, 0, 2, 2, 4) rows, then 1 stitch at the beginning

of the next 6 (8, 10, 12, 16, 18) rows—79 (82, 85, 84, 85, 84) stitches remain.

Bind off all remaining stitches.

## Finishing

Weave in all the ends. Block all pieces to the finished measurements.

Sew the shoulder seams.

Set in the sleeves.

Sew the side and sleeve seams.

## Buttonhole Band

Mark the left front edge for 6 buttonholes, with the bottom button about ½" (13mm) above the bottom edge, and the top button at the start of the neck shaping. Evenly space the remaining 4 buttons in between.

With the circular needle and the right side facing, begin at the lower right front, pick up and knit 82 (84, 86, 90, 92, 96) stitches along the right front to the beginning of the neck shaping, 48 (49, 50, 49, 49, 48) stitches along the right neck, 27 (29, 31, 33, 35, 37) stitches along the back neck, 48 (49, 50, 49, 49, 48) stitches along the left neck, then 82 (84, 86, 90, 92, 96) stitches along the left front to the bottom edge—287 (295, 303, 311, 317, 325) stitches.

Work in the k1, p1 rib pattern for 3 rows.

NEXT ROW (RS): Continue in rib, making buttonholes on the left front side as follows: *Work in the rib pattern to the first buttonhole marker, yarn over twice, k2tog through the back of the

loops; repeat from * 5 more times, then work in the pattern to the end of the row.

NEXT ROW: *Work in the rib pattern to the first double yarn over, drop the first yarn over from the needle, work the second yarn over in rib to match the pattern; repeat from * 5 more times, then continue in the pattern to the end of the row.

Continue in the k1, p1 rib pattern for 3 more rows. Bind off all the stitches in the pattern.

Sew the buttons to the right front band opposite the buttonholes.

---

## MAKE IT MORE FEMININE

While deep blue is great for a guy, if you're going to make this for a woman, try knitting it up in 7519 English Manor (top) or 7511 Slate Green (bottom).

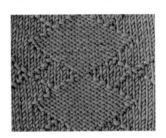

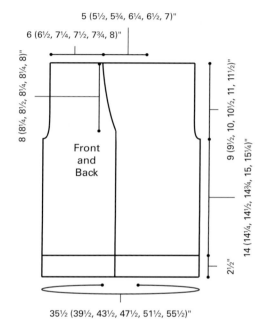

5 (5½, 5¾, 6¼, 6½, 7)"

6 (6½, 7¼, 7½, 7¾, 8)"

8 (8¼, 8½, 8¼, 8¼, 8)"

Front and Back

9 (9½, 10, 10½, 11, 11½)"

14 (14¼, 14½, 14¾, 15, 15¼)"

2½"

35½ (39½, 43½, 47½, 51½, 55½)"

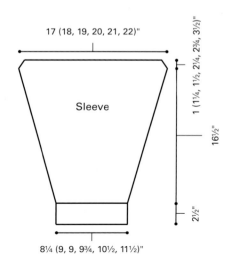

17 (18, 19, 20, 21, 22)"

Sleeve

1 (1¼, 1½, 2¼, 2¾, 3½)"

16½"

2½"

8¼ (9, 9, 9¾, 10½, 11½)"

## ARGYLE PANEL

(panel 23 sts)

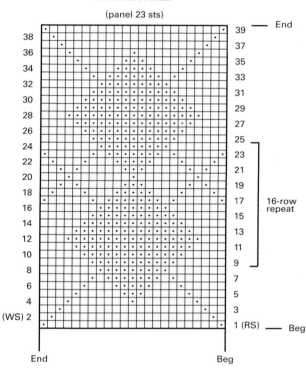

End

39
37
35
33
31
29
27
25
23
21
19
17
15
13
11
9
7
5
3
1 (RS) — Beg

38
36
34
32
30
28
26
24
22
20
18
16
14
12
10
8
6
4
(WS) 2

16-row repeat

End

Beg

### STITCH KEY

☐  = Knit on RS, purl on WS

⊡  = Purl on RS, knit on WS

# Honeycomb Pullover

This pullover is right out of the pages of an Italian fashion magazine—chic and casual, perfect for an afternoon at the country club or the mall. Stitch definition is everything in this 3-dimensional fabric, and fixing mistakes is tricky. So check your work every few rows to avoid disaster.

**Skill Level** ▶ Intermediate

## Finished Measurements

| Woman's Size | Man's Size | Bust/Chest | Length |
|---|---|---|---|
| S | XS | 34½" (87.5cm) | 24" (61cm) |
| M | S | 39" (99cm) | 24½" (62cm) |
| L | M | 42½" (108cm) | 25" (63.5cm) |
| XL | L | 47" (119.5cm) | 25½" (65cm) |
| XXL | XL | 50" (127cm) | 26¼" (66.5cm) |
| XXXL | XXL | 54½" (138cm) | 27" (68.5cm) |

If only one number is used, it applies to all sizes.
Pictured in size Women's Medium in Willow; Men's Medium in Sandalwood

## Materials
- Louet Gems (100% merino wool, each approximately 3½ oz [50g], 175 yd [160m]), 8 (9, 10, 11, 12, 13) skeins in color 44 Sandalwood or 55 Willow, (**3**) light
- One pair size U.S. 6 (4mm) knitting needles, or size needed to obtain gauge
- Size U.S. 6 (4mm) 16" (40cm) circular needle
- Stitch markers
- Blunt-tip yarn needle

## Gauge
21 stitches and 40 rows = 4" (10cm) in slipped honeycomb pattern
To save time, take time to check gauge.

## Stitch Patterns
**Rib Pattern** *(odd number stitches)*
ROW 1 (WS): K1, *p1, k1; repeat from * to the end.
ROW 2: P1, *k1, p1; repeat from * to the end.
Repeat Rows 1 and 2 for the pattern.

**Slipped Honeycomb Pattern**
*(multiple of 4 stitches + 1)*
ROW 1 AND ALL OTHER WRONG-SIDE ROWS: Purl.
ROWS 2 AND 4 (RS): K1, *slip 3 purlwise one at a time with yarn in front, k1; repeat from * to the end.
ROW 6: K1, *k1, insert right needle under and behind the strands across the front of the 2 previous right-side rows, then knit into the next stitch, lifting and catching the 2 strands, k2; repeat from * to the end.
ROWS 8 AND 10: K3, *slip 3 purlwise one at a time with yarn in front, k1; repeat from * to the last 2 stitches, end k2.
ROW 12: K3, *k1, insert right needle under and behind the strands across the front of the 2 previous right-side rows, then knit into the next stitch, lifting and catching the 2 strands, k2; repeat from * to the last 2 stitches, k2.
Repeat Rows 1–12 for the pattern.

## Back

Have you knit your gauge swatch in the honeycomb pattern?

Okay then.

With the straight needles, cast on 87 (99, 107, 119, 127, 139) sts.

Work in the rib pattern until the piece measures about 2¾" (7cm) from the cast-on edge, ending with a right-side row.

NEXT ROW (WS): Work in the rib pattern and increase 6 stitches evenly spaced across the row—93 (105, 113, 125, 133, 145) stitches.

Begin the slipped honeycomb pattern and work even until the piece measures 14½ (14½, 15, 15, 15¾, 16)" (37 [37, 38, 38, 40, 40.5] cm) from the cast-on edge. Place a marker on each side of the piece to mark for the armholes.

Continue to work even until the armhole measures 9½ (10, 10, 10½, 10½, 11)" (24 [25.5, 25.5, 26.5, 26.5, 28]cm) from the armhole markers, ending with a wrong-side row and Row 1 or 7 of the slipped honeycomb pattern.

Bind off all stitches.

Place a marker 30 (35, 38, 43, 46, 51) stitches from each side for the shoulders, leaving the center 33 (35, 37, 39, 41, 43) stitches for the back neck.

## Front

Work the same as the Back until the armhole measures 6½ (7, 6¾, 7¼, 7, 7½)" (16.5 [18, 17, 18.5, 18, 19]cm), ending with a wrong-side row, and Row 1 or 7 of the slipped honeycomb pattern.

### SHAPE NECK

Work in pattern across 40 (45, 48, 53, 56, 61) stitches, join a second ball of yarn, bind off the center 13 (15, 17, 19, 21, 23) stitches for the neck, work in pattern across the remaining 40 (45, 48, 53, 56, 61) stitches.

Work both sides at once with separate balls of yarn.

NEXT ROW (WS): Purl to 2 stitches before neck edge, p2tog; p2tog at the beginning of the other side of the neck, purl to the end—1 stitch decreased on each side of the neck.

Continue decreasing 1 stitch at each neck edge on wrong-side rows every 4 rows 5 times more;

decrease 1 stitch at each neck edge every wrong-side row 4 times—30 (35, 38, 43, 46, 51) stitches remain for each side. Work even in the pattern until piece measures 24 (24½, 25, 25½, 26¼, 27)" (61 [61.5, 63.5, 64.5, 68.5]cm) from the cast-on edge, ending with a wrong-side row and Row 1 or 7 of the slipped honeycomb pattern.

Bind off the remaining stitches.

## Sleeves (Make 2)

With the straight needles, cast on 45 (49, 49, 53, 57, 61) stitches.

Work in the rib pattern until the piece measures 2" (5cm) from

the back neck edge—96 (100, 108, 112, 120, 124) stitches. Place a marker for the beginning of the round, and join.

ROUND 1: *K1, p1; repeat from * around. Repeat this round for 1¼" (3cm) or until the neckband is the desired length. Bind off loosely in pattern.

Sew the sleeves to the body between the armhole markers.

Sew the side and sleeve seams. If desired, lightly steam-block the seams.

## MAKE IT GENDER NEUTRAL

Use 43 Pewter for a sweater you can both wear comfortably in any situation.

the cast-on edge, ending with a right-side row.

Begin the slipped honeycomb pattern. *At the same time,* increase 1 stitch on each side of every right-side row 6 (6, 6, 6, 4, 6) times, every 6 rows 7 (7, 7, 14, 12, 10) times, then every 8 rows 15 (15, 15, 10, 12, 12) times, working the new stitches into the pattern when there are enough stitches on each side for a repeat—101 (105, 105, 113, 113, 117) stitches.

Work even until the piece measures 20 (20, 20, 20, 20, 19½)" (51 [51, 51, 51, 51, 49.5]cm) from the cast-on edge. Bind off all stitches.

## Finishing

Weave in all ends. Do not block the pieces.

Sew the shoulder seams.

## Neckband

With the right side facing, using the circular needle and beginning at the left shoulder seam, pick up and knit 20 (20, 22, 22, 24, 24) stitches along the left neck edge, 13 (15, 17, 19, 21, 23) stitches along the front bound-off edge, 20 (20, 22, 22, 24, 24) stitches along the right neck edge, and 43 (45, 47, 49, 51, 53) stitches along

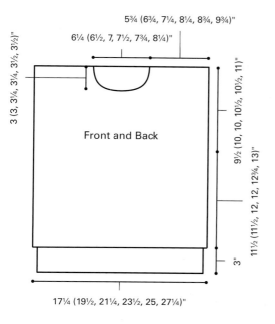

5¾ (6¾, 7¼, 8¼, 8¾, 9¾)"

6¼ (6½, 7, 7½, 7¾, 8¼)"

3 (3, 3¼, 3¼, 3½, 3½)"

Front and Back

9½ (10, 10, 10½, 10½, 11)"

11½ (11½, 12, 12, 12¾, 13)"

3"

17¼ (19½, 21¼, 23½, 25, 27¼)"

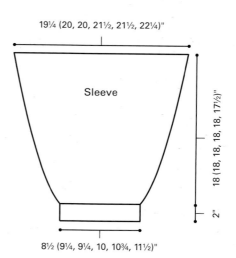

19¼ (20, 20, 21½, 21½, 22¼)"

Sleeve

18 (18, 18, 18, 18, 17½)"

2"

8½ (9¼, 9¼, 10, 10¾, 11½)"

## SLIPPED HONEYCOMB PATTERN

(mult 4 + 1 sts)

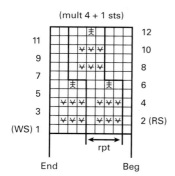

rpt

End          Beg

*The odd numbers are on the left side of this chart since you begin the chart with a wrong-side row. But please, as always, read each row of this chart from right to left.*

## STITCH KEY

☐ = Knit

⋎ = Slip st purlwise with yarn in front

ⵏ = Insert RH needle under and behind the strands across the front of the 2 previous right-side rows, then into the next stitch on the LH needle, pulling loop of the new stitch down behind the loose strands, then up in front of the strands before dropping the old stitch from the left-hand needle and catching the strands behind the new stitch

# MERINO, SILK, AND **DUCK CONFIT**

It was the first cold evening of fall when my partner, Mark, and I made the two-hour drive into New York for dinner. As much as I loved living in the country, I missed autumn in New York. That night, we planned on a quiet walk through the West Village after dinner at a tiny French bistro we loved on Cornelia Street.

Le Gigot, with its deep yellow-orange paint, mirrored bar, and hard bent-wood chairs, looked like it was lifted straight out of the Left Bank in Paris. On the wall, just inside the French doors we passed through, was a row of Shaker-style pegs. They were all but hidden under four layers of coats. I added my black alpaca jacket to the expanding mass of cloth, but Mark was hesitant to add his scarf—over five feet of tightly knit linen stitch in Manos Silk Blend that I had just finished for him that morning. It was thin but warm, and richly textured as if it had just left the loom. I convinced him to put it on the wall rather than have it stained with food—or worse, knocked about and walked on in the tiny dining room. I was hoping at least for a table where I could keep an eye on my latest work of art.

We were seated at the back, as far from the coat hooks as possible. I drowned my fears in a bottle of 1990 Provencal Gigondas and duck confit cassoulet. Dinner was all I had hoped it would be, until the owner, a thin, redheaded Parisian ex-pat, came by the table to see if we were enjoying dinner. She was wearing Mark's scarf, wrapped loosely around her shoulders like a wide cowl—the breath caught in my throat as I tried to make sense of the situation. With his back to her, Mark assumed I was choking on a duck bone and started to rush around the table to administer the Heimlich maneuver. Then he saw the scarf around her shoulders and suddenly it looked as if he might try the Heimlich on her, though closer to her neck than her abdomen.

When we all calmed down, she told us that she had admired it on the coat pegs and decided to wear it, hoping to buy it from the owner, who would no doubt notice that she had it on.

"It's not for sale," Mark said. "He made it."

"How much do you want to make me one?"

"You can't afford it." I said.

The yarn she could afford, it was my time that was off-limits. We all know how long it takes to knit more than five feet of DK weight yarn. Then it struck me: a barter.

"Would you trade another dinner for a scarf?" I asked as she ran off, still wearing Mark's scarf, to deal with a table across the room. Mark thought I was nuts.

"It took you so long to knit that one," he said. But then he took a bite of his duck.

All thoughts about my welfare went out the window as he filled both of our glasses with more Gigondas.

"How many courses?" she asked when she returned to our table.

"Four. And two bottles of wine."

"My choice," Mark butted in.

We negotiated on and off during the rest of our meal and in the end struck a happy bargain.

Mark tends to like one-of-a-kinds when it comes to what I knit for him, but luckily for the both of us, he likes cassoulet with duck confit even more.

# 3.

# REVERSIBILITY

Most men just don't pay attention to how they get dressed. Sweaters get thrown on backward and cabled scarves are thrown every which way, hiding your gorgeous work from the world. These patterns take care of all those problems with a few more challenging techniques, including double knitting and reversible cables. Plus, many of these projects are small accessories, helping you avoid any dreaded curses that might come with a sweater.

# DOUBLE KNITTING

Double knitting is a two-color technique that is most remarkable for its reversible design—each side mirrors the other with the colors reversed. This technique creates two pieces of stockinette fabric situated back-to-back with their wrong (or purl) sides facing each other and their right (or knit) sides facing out. The two pieces are interlocked so they won't separate and form one extra thick piece of fabric.

Two balls of yarn are carried across each and every row. And since two pieces of fabric are being knit at once, both yarns are used for every stitch—at each stitch one is used to knit the front fabric and the other is used to purl the back fabric. By switching which yarn is knit and which is purled, the colors reverse and two pieces become interlocked.

Since you are knitting two pieces of fabric at once, you must cast twice as many stitches as you see on either side. A scarf that is 6" wide with 4 stitches per inch requires 48 stitches cast on for the entire scarf—24 stitches for each side.

### Easy Double-Knit Cast-On

Hold both yarns together and cast on over 2 needles at once using whatever method you prefer (long tail, knit cast-on, etc.). Since each cast-on stitch will provide two loops (one for each strand held together), you only cast on the number of stitches needed for one side. Your cast-on edge will now have the correct number of loops in alternating colors. Why use two needles at once? Pull one out after the cast-on, and you'll have stitches loose enough to manipulate with ease. The only drawback with this cast-on method is that both colors will be visible at the bottom and top edges of your scarf. But the upside is that it's really easy to do—and since you're adding heavy fringe in the Double-Knit Double-Knot Scarf (page 90) you won't notice the edges all that much.

### Long Tail–Style Double-Knit Cast-On

Make a slipknot, using both yarns held together, with a 6-inch tail. Separate the two yarns and hold them as you would for a long tail cast-on, that is,

one yarn over your thumb and the other over your index finger. Cast on 1 stitch in the long-tail manner—this stitch will appear on the needle from the yarn that was over your index finger. Now let go of both yarns and reverse them so that the one that was over your thumb is now over your index finger and vice versa. Cast on your second stitch in the regular long-tail manner, and you will see the second stitch appear in the second color. Reverse the yarns back to their original positions without twisting them and continue to cast on the desired number of stitches. Do not count the slipknot as a stitch. After working your first row, drop the slipknot. The advantage to this cast-on method is that the edges are more even, with the colors lying on one side or the other. But it is a bit more complicated and requires some practice.

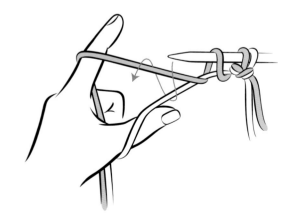

### Decreasing in Double Knitting

In double knitting, the knit stitches will be decreased as k2tog and the purl stitches will be decreased as p2tog. Since each knit stitch (representing the outside layer) is separated by a purl stitch (which represent the inside layer), you must rearrange the stitches so that the 2 knits are next to each other and the 2 purls are next to each other before you can decrease.

When you arrive at your first decrease:

1. Slip the first stitch (k) as if to purl.

2. Slip the second stitch (p) as if to purl to a cable needle and hold in back.

3. Slip the third stitch (k) as if to purl.

4. Slip the stitch on the cable needle back to the left-hand needle, taking care not to twist it.

5. Slip the 2 knit stitches on the right-hand needle back to the left-hand needle, taking care not to twist them.

6. K2tog then p2tog.

Repeat this process every time you need to decrease in double knitting.

# REVERSIBLE CABLES

Cables are simply stitches that were knit out of order (page 22). When knit in stockinette, there is clearly a front and back side to them, which is great for sweaters, but not for scarves. To make them reversible, start with ribs. Ribbing looks the same on both sides and cabling within an even rib (k1, p1; k2, p2; k3, p3; etc.), will result in a cable that looks exactly the same on both sides. The fun and challenge come from using multiple cables of different widths, twisting them on different rows, some touching and some separated with noncabled stitches between them. The possibilities are endless. See the Reverse Cable Scarf (page 88) for one possible pattern demonstrating this concept.

## KITCHENER STITCH

Kitchener stitch weaves two open edges together with a fairly invisible seam. Use it to bind off two layers of double knitting.

Thread your yarn needle with a length of yarn 4 times the length of the seam you are trying to weave together.

**Setup:** Holding both pieces together, lining them up stitch by stitch with the pointed ends of the needles facing right, and working right to left, insert yarn needle into the first stitch on the front needle as if to purl, pull the yarn through, leaving the stitch on the needle. Insert yarn needle into first stitch on the back needle as if to knit, pull the yarn through and leave the stitch on the needle.

1. Insert the yarn needle into the first stitch on the front needle as if to knit, pull the yarn through and take the stitch off.

2. Insert the yarn needle into the first stitch on the front needle as if to purl, pull the yarn through and leave the stitch on.

3. Insert the yarn needle into the first stitch on the back needle as if to purl, pull the yarn through and take the stitch off.

4. Insert the yarn needle into the first stitch on the back needle as if to knit, pull the yarn through and leave the stitch on.

Repeat these 4 steps until 1 stitch remains on each needle, cut yarn, and pass it through both stitches to fasten. Weave in end.

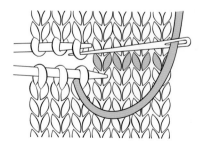

# HERRINGBONE STITCH

This stitch not only captures the diagonal lines of herringbone on each side, but each side is completely different. Just like stockinette, this stitch calls for knitting one row and purling the next. But that's where the similarity ends.

## On the Knit Side

On the knit side of the fabric, you will ssk (slip, slip, knit) every stitch. Since ssk is a decrease stitch that involves knitting two stitches together, you will only drop one of those stitches off the left-hand needle after knitting them to avoid reducing the total number of stitches. To get a sense of how and why, let's first take a close look at what ssk actually does.

1. Slip the first stitch from the left-hand needle as if to knit.

2. Slip the second stitch from the left-hand needle as if to knit. Slipping the stitches as if to knit turns them around, facing them toward the back.

3. Put them both back on the left-hand needle in their new orientation and knit them together through the back loops—but don't drop them from the left-hand needle.

4. Drop only the first stitch from the left-hand needle to keep the stitch count the same. Your left-hand needle is still connected to a piece of the last stitch. Count that loop as the new first stitch on the left-hand needle. But since it was part of the previous ssk it has already been turned. Time for the next ssk.

5. Slip this first stitch on the left-hand needle as if to knit, keeping in mind that it is already turned so it will appear that you are slipping it as if to knit from the back.

6. Slip the second stitch on the left-hand needle in the normal manner as if to knit.

7. Put them both back on the left-hand needle in their new orientation and knit them together through the back loops—but only drop the first one off the left-hand needle, as you did before.

This repeats down the row until only one stitch remains. Knit this stitch.

## On the Purl Side

Purl two stitches together in the normal manner, but only drop the first stitch off the left-hand needle. One stitch will still be connected to the left-hand needle—this is the first stitch in your next purl two together. Continue down the row until only 1 stitch remains and purl that last stitch.

Reversible
Cable Scarf

# Reversible Cable Scarf

Two pairs of cables, each turned on a different row, give this scarf plenty of movement, like a waterfall of yarn. This is a thick, soft, and warm scarf that he's not going to share willingly, so be prepared to make two of them right from the start.

**Skill Level** ▶ Intermediate

**Finished Measurements**
Width 8" (20.5cm)
Length 72" (183cm)

## Materials
- Cascade Yarns Eco Duo (70% undyed baby alpaca, 30% undyed merino wool, each approximately 3½ oz (100g) and 197 yd [180m], 5 skeins in color 1701 Zebra, 1704 Chicory, or 1703 Storm, **(4)** medium
- One pair size U.S. 9 (5.5mm) needles, or size needed to obtain gauge
- Cable needle
- Blunt-tip yarn needle

## Gauge
48 stitches and 23 rows = 4" (10cm) in cabled rib pattern
To save time, take time to check gauge. Row gauge is less important on this pattern as you just knit until the scarf is long enough.

## Stitch Pattern
K2, P2 Rib *(multiple of 4 stitches)*
ROW 1: *P2, k2; repeat from * across.
Repeat Row 1.

## Scarf
Cast on 96 stitches.

Work in k2, p2 rib for 6 rows.

CABLE ROW 1 (RS): *Slip 12 stitches to a cable needle and hold in front, (p2, k2) 3 times, (p2, k2) 3 times from the cable needle, work 24 stitches in the established pattern; repeat from * across.

Work 5 rows in k2, p2 rib.

CABLE ROW 2 (RS): *Work 24 stitches in the established pattern, slip the next 12 stitches to a cable needle and hold in front, (p2, k2) 3 times, (p2, k2) 3 times from the cable needle; repeat from * across.

Work 5 rows in k2, p2 rib.

Repeat the last 12 rows until the scarf is approximately 71½" (181.5cm), ending with either Cable row 1 or Cable row 2. Work 3 rows in k2, p2 rib. Bind off in pattern.

## Finishing
Weave in all ends. Do not block.

## MAKE IT MORE NEUTRAL

For a more conservative guy, try this scarf in color 1704 Chicory (top) or 1703 Storm (bottom).

## REVERSIBLE CABLE SCARF **CHART**

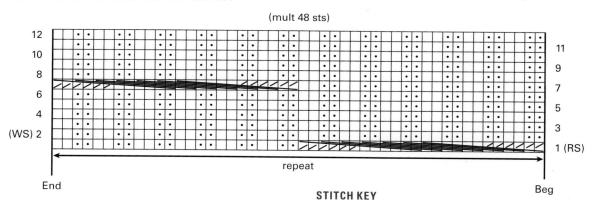

(mult 48 sts)

repeat

End                                                                 Beg

**STITCH KEY**

☐ = K on RS; p on WS

• = P on RS; k on WS

⟋⟋⟋ = Slip 12 sts onto cn and hold in front,
(p2, k2) 3 times, (p2, k2) 3 times from cn

# Double-Knit Double-Knot Scarf

Inspired by medieval and Moorish design motifs, this reversible scarf has a heavy fringe that will look great on you, but some men may object to it. For those guys, simply leave the fringe off, which will make the scarf that much easier and faster to complete.

**Skill Level** Advanced

### Finished Measurements
Width 9" (23cm)
Length 71" (180cm) without fringe

### Materials
- Knit One Crochet Too Second Time Cotton (75% recycled cotton, 25% acrylic, each approximately 3½ oz [100g] and 180 yds [165m], 3 skeins in color 478 Brick or 534 Artichoke and 5 skeins 485 Ochre or 855 Earth, (4) medium
- 3 size U.S. 6 (4 mm) straight needles, or size needed to obtain gauge
- Size U.S. G-6 (4mm) crochet hook

### Gauge
20 sts and 26 rows = 4" (10cm) in stockinette stitch
To save time, take time to check gauge.

## Scarf

Cast on 90 stitches using your choice of double-knit cast-on (see page 84).

Begin working from chart, repeating Rows 3–16 35 times or until scarf measures about 70½" (179cm).

Work Row 17.

## Binding Off

You will bind off by grafting the front and back layers together.

Start by slipping all the stitches from the current needle to the other 2 straight needles in this fashion: slip all the knit stitches (as if to purl) to one needle and all the purl stitches (as if to purl) to the other needle. This takes a little dexterity as you alternate one stitch to one needle, the next to the other and so on and so forth down the row. Use the Kitchener stitch (page 85) to graft the stitches from both needles. Once all the stitches are grafted, secure the yarn by doing a few duplicate embroidery stitches over the same colors as the tails you're weaving in and then slip the excess in between the front and back pieces of fabric.

## Fringe

You will make a total of 24 fringes.

### SETUP
For each fringe, cut 20 18"-long (45.5cm) pieces of yarn in either Ochre or Earth; 240 strands— keep each bunch separate.

Mark where your fringes will go, starting 1 stitch in from each end and spacing 12 fringes evenly across.

REVERSIBILITY

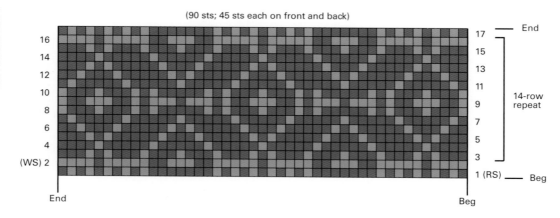

(90 sts; 45 sts each on front and back)

14-row repeat

**COLOR KEY**

■ = A

■ = B

**STITCH KEY**

□ = K color shown and p color not shown on RS; k color not shown and p color shown on WS

Each square in the pattern represents 2 stitches—one for the layer facing you and one for the layer behind.

There is only one color in each square to make the chart easier to read.

The other color is there, hidden behind the one you see, creating a reverse image on the back side.

- On odd-numbered rows, knit the color you see in each square (creating the front layer) then purl the color you don't see in each square (creating the back layer).
- On even-numbered rows, knit the color you don't *see* in each square then purl the color you see in each square.

Remember, it's important to bring both yarns to the front as you knit and both yarns to the back as you purl.

## ATTACHING THE FRINGE

Grab one bunch of strands and fold them in half, keeping the looped end open. Insert your crochet hook from back to front where you've marked for the first stitch, and slip the massive loop of strands over the hook and pull them through the scarf. Use the hook or your fingers to pull the back end of all 40 strands, en masse, through the loop you pulled through the scarf. Gently pull to tighten. Then gently pull each individual strand to get the knot tight and fat where the fringe meets the scarf.

Attach all 12 fringes evenly spaced as marked.

## MAKING THE FIRST JOIN

After all 12 fringes are put on one side, make your life easier by gathering all the strands in each fringe separately, and binding them with a twist tie or paper clip about 7" (18cm) down.

Join the first two fringes 1" (2.5cm) down from the top knot using a 1-yard length of yarn. Wind around 10 times then use a blunt-tip tapestry needle to secure the end inside the new knot. Continue down the row, joining 2 fringes together and at the same level, creating 6 new "knots."

## MAKING THE SECOND JOIN

Leave the first fringe alone and join the second and third fringe in the same manner as above, 1" (2.5cm) below the last join. Note that this join will be spaced in between the previous joins. It's best to remove the twist ties or paper clips only as you get to them. Once the second row of 5 knots is complete, trim all the edges even with scissors 2" (5cm) below the second knot. Repeat on the other end of the scarf.

## TYING THE KNOT

Tying the fringes together can be a slow process. To speed things up, fold your yard of yarn in half. Slip it under the 2 fringes being joined just where you want it. Slip the 2 loose ends of your tying strand through the loop at the other end that was formed when you folded it in half. Pull to tighten the yarn in position, locking the two fringes together. Wrap the doubled strand around and around the 2 clumps of fringe until just a few inches remain. Thread these ends into a blunt yarn needle and fasten off by pulling the ends up through the bottom of the newly formed knot, tightening and trimming it so the ends disappear.

## MAKE IT MORE MASCULINE

The fringe on this scarf is dramatic—maybe too dramatic for some guys. In that case, leave the fringe off and go with more subdued colors like 855 Earth and 534 Artichoke.

# Reversible Paisley Hat

Double knitting in the round is easier than double knitting flat since you're always looking at the same side while knitting. The turned-up brim shows off what's happening with color on both sides.

**Skill Level** ▶ Advanced

## Sizes
S/M (L/XL)

## Finished Measurements
Circumference 19½ (24½)" (49.5 [62]cm)

## Materials
- Cascade 220, 100% Peruvian highland wool, 3½ oz (100g), 220yd (201m), 1 (1) skein color Pistachio #8234 (A), and 1 (1) skein color Jet #4002 (B), **4** medium
- Set of 5 size 7 (3.5 mm) double pointed needles
- Stitch marker
- Two blunt-end yarn needles

## Gauge
36 stitches and 22 rows = 4" (10cm) in double knitting pattern; 18 stitches will show on the front, and the other 18 stitches are on the back.
To save time, take time to check gauge.

## Hat

With Color A over your index finger and Color B over your thumb, cast on 176 (220) stitches; 88 (110) stitches will be worked for the outer layer of the hat, and the remaining 88 (110) stitches will be worked for the inner layer of the hat. Join to work in the round, being careful not to twist the stitches. Place a marker for the beginning of the round.

▶ **Size M only:**
ROUND 1: Begin chart on Row 6, and work first 44 stitches twice.

Continue even through Row 53.

▶ **Size L only:**
ROUND 1: Begin chart on Row 1 and work first 44 stitches twice, then work the remaining 22 stitches.

Continue even through Row 53.

**SHAPING CROWN:**
Crown shaping requires decreasing by knitting two together for the front side and purling 2 together for the reverse side. See page 85 for the details on setting up the stitches in double knitting for knitting and purling 2 together.

ROUND 54: * K2tog on the outer layer, p2tog on the inner layer, work the next 18 stitches (9 stitches for the outer layer and 9 stitches for the inner layer)

according to the chart; repeat from * to the end of the round—160 (200) stitches remain.

**ROUND 55 AND ALL ODD ROUNDS TO ROUND 69:** Work even according to the chart.

**ROUND 56:** *K2tog on the outer layer, p2tog on the inner layer, work the next 16 stitches (8 stitches for the outer layer and 8 stitches for the inner layer) according to the chart; repeat from * to the end of the round—144 (180) stitches remain.

**ROUND 58:** *K2tog on the outer layer, p2tog on the inner layer, work the next 14 stitches according to the chart; repeat from * to the end of the round—128 (160) stitches remain.

**ROUND 60:** *K2tog on the outer layer, p2tog on the inner layer, work the next 12 stitches according to the chart; repeat from * to the end of the round—112 (140) stitches remain.

**ROUND 62:** *K2tog on the outer layer, p2tog on the inner layer, work the next 10 stitches according to the chart; repeat from * to the end of the round—96 (120) stitches remain.

**ROUND 64:** *K2tog on the outer layer, p2tog on the inner layer, work the next 8 stitches according to the chart; repeat from * to the end of the round—80 (100) stitches remain.

**ROUND 66:** *K2tog on the outer layer, p2tog on the inner layer, work the next 6 stitches according to the chart; repeat from * to the end of the round—64 (80) stitches remain.

**ROUND 68:** *K2tog on the outer layer, p2tog on the inner layer, work the next 4 stitches according to the chart; repeat from * to the end of the round—48 (60) stitches remain.

**ROUND 70:** *K2tog on the outer layer, p2tog on the inner layer, work the next 2 stitches according to the chart; repeat from * to the end of the round—32 (40) stitches remain.

**ROUND 71:** *K2tog on the outer layer, p2tog on the inner layer; repeat from * to the end of the round—16 (20) stitches remain.

## Finishing

Thread the first blunt-end yarn needle with A, and slip through all remaining color A stitches, moving clockwise around the needles, leaving all the stitches on the needles. Using a second blunt-end yarn needle, repeat with B.

Remove the double-pointed needles, making sure A is at the outside of the hat and B is at the inside of the hat.

Pull each needle to tighten and close the top of the hat. Secure each yarn and tuck in between the layers to hide.

## REVERSIBLE PAISLEY HAT **CHART**

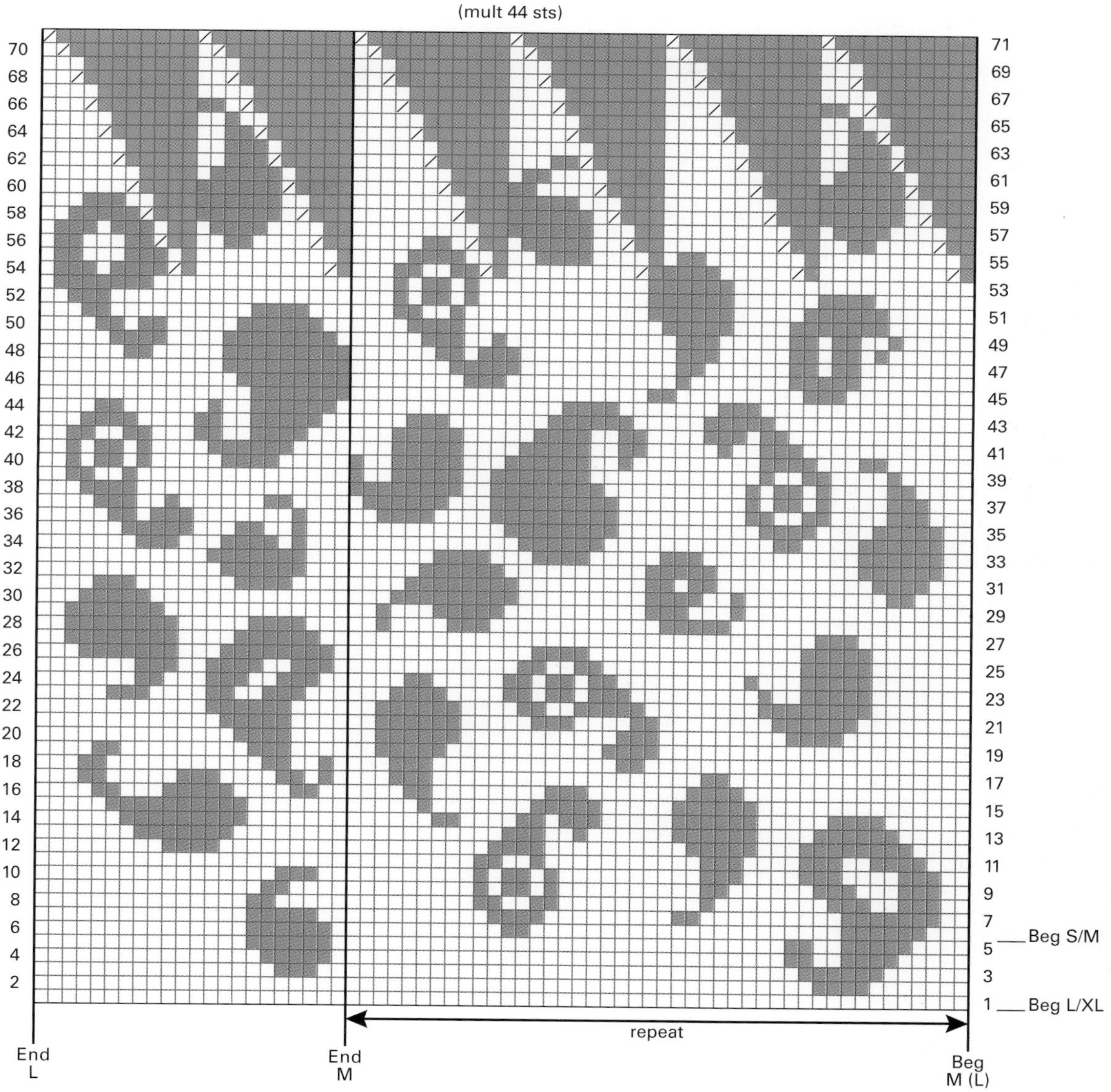
(mult 44 sts)
Beg S/M
Beg L/XL
repeat
End L
End M
Beg M (L)

**COLOR KEY**

- ▒ = A for outer layer; B for inner layer
- ☐ = B for outer layer; A for inner layer

**STITCH KEY**

- ☐ = K for outer layer; p for inner layer
- ⧄ = K2tog for outer layer; p2tog for inner layer
- ▒ = No stitch

# **Boat Neck** Faux Rib Pullover

The beauty of this supersoft wide-neck pullover is that it just doesn't matter how it's worn. Front to back it's exactly the same. Inside out, the faux ribs offer a really nice texture and the exposed seams give a deconstructed look that's very downtown.

**Skill Level** Easy

## Finished Measurements

| Woman's Size | Man's Size | Bust/Chest | Length |
|---|---|---|---|
| S | XS | 37½" (95cm) | 25¼" (64cm) |
| M | S | 41½" (105.5cm) | 26" (66cm) |
| L | M | 45½" (115.5cm) | 26¾" (68cm) |
| XL | L | 49½" (125.5cm) | 27½" (70cm) |
| XXL | XL | 53½" (136cm) | 28¼" (72cm) |
| XXXL | XXL | 57½" (146cm) | 29" (74cm) |

If only one number is used, it applies to all sizes.

## Materials
- Lion Brand LBCollection Baby Alpaca (100% baby alpaca, each approximately 1¾ oz [50g], 146 yd [133m]), 12 (13, 14, 15, 17, 18) balls color 124 Tan, **(3)** light
- One pair size U.S. 4 (3.5mm) straight needles, or size needed to obtain gauge
- Size U.S. 4 (3.5mm) double-pointed needles, set of 5, or size needed to obtain gauge
- Stitch holders
- Blunt-tip yarn needle

## Gauge
28 stitches and 40 rows = 4" (10cm) in faux rib pattern
To save time, take time to check gauge.

## Stitch Pattern
Faux Rib
ROW 1 (RS): P1,*slip 1 with yarn in back, p1; repeat from * to the end.
ROW 2 (WS): Purl.
Repeat Rows 1 and 2 for the pattern.

## Back

With the straight needles, cast on 133 (147, 161, 175, 189, 203) stitches.

Work in the faux rib pattern until the piece measures 24 (24¾, 25¼, 26, 26½, 27¼)" (61 [63, 64, 66, 67.5, 69]cm) from the cast-on edge, ending with a wrong-side row.

### SHAPE NECK
NEXT ROW (RS): Work 41 (47, 53, 59, 65, 71) stitches, bind off the center 51 (53, 55, 57, 59, 61) stitches in the established pattern, work remaining 41 (47, 53, 59, 65, 71) stitches.

### LEFT SHOULDER
Work Faux Rib pattern for 2 rows even.

Place the remaining stitches on a holder.

### RIGHT SHOULDER
With the wrong side facing, attach yarn to begin with a wrong-side row. Work Faux Rib pattern for 2 rows even.

Place the remaining stitches on a holder.

## Front

Work the same as the Back.

## Sleeves (Make 2)

With the straight needles, cast on 69 (71, 75, 79, 83, 85) stitches.

Work in the faux rib pattern until the piece measures 2" (5cm) from the cast-on edge, ending with a wrong-side row.

Increase 1 stitch at each end of this row, every 4 rows 26 (36, 30, 32, 30, 35) times, then every 6 rows 12 (5, 9, 8, 8, 5) times— 147 (155, 155, 161, 161, 167) stitches. Work the new stitches into the pattern.

---

┌─ MAKE IT MORE MASCULINE ─────────────────────

In tan, this sweater is gender-neutral. Make it in 126 Auburn (left) or 152 Silver Gray Heather (right) for the more mature man in your life. And give him a contrasting new collared shirt to wear under it.

Continue even until the piece measures 20 (20, 20, 20, 19½, 19½)" (51 [51, 51, 51, 49.5, 49.5] cm) from the cast-on edge, ending with a right-side row.

Bind off purlwise.

## Finishing

Weave in all ends. Do not block the pieces.

Place the shoulder stitches on the double-pointed needles. Holding the Front and Back with the right sides together, join the shoulders using a 3-needle bind-off.

Sew the Sleeves to the Front and Back, placing the center of the sleeve at the shoulder seam and making sure the ends of the sleeve are evenly spaced on both sides of the body. Sew the side and sleeve seams.

## BOAT NECK FAUX RIB PULLOVER **SCHEMATIC AND CHART**

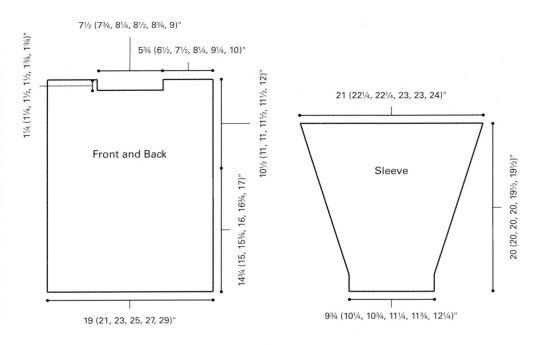

7½ (7¾, 8¼, 8½, 8¾, 9)"

5¾ (6½, 7½, 8¼, 9¼, 10)"

1¼ (1¼, 1½, 1½, 1¾, 1¾)"

Front and Back

10½ (11, 11, 11½, 11½, 12)"

14¾ (15, 15¾, 16, 16¾, 17)"

19 (21, 23, 25, 27, 29)"

21 (22¼, 22¼, 23, 23, 24)"

Sleeve

20 (20, 20, 20, 19½, 19½)"

9¾ (10¼, 10¾, 11¼, 11¾, 12¼)"

**FAUX RIB**

(mult 2 + 1 sts)

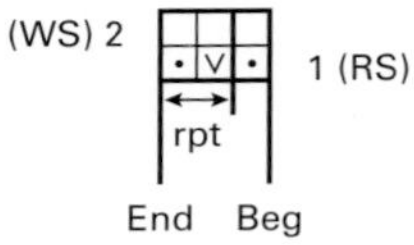

(WS) 2 | | · | V | · | | 1 (RS)

rpt

End    Beg

**STITCH KEY**

☐ = Knit on RS, purl on WS

· = Purl on RS, knit on WS

V = Slip st purlwise with yarn in back

# **Reversible** Herringbone Scarf

Don't be put off by the large number of stitches to cast on, since you're knitting this scarf the long way. But do give yourself enough time to finish a row when you pick up your project. Stopping in the middle of any row in this stitch pattern is dangerous because stitches can accidentally fall off the needle when you set it down. And the only way to fix dropped stitches in this stitch pattern is to unknit all the way back to the problem. If you must stop in the middle of a row, put point protectors on your needles to keep the stitches from falling off.

**Skill Level** Intermediate

### Finished Measurements
Width 7" (18cm)
Length 90" (229cm)

### Materials
- Karabella Super Yak (50% yak, 50% superfine merino wool, each approximately 1¾ oz [50g] and 125 yd [114m]), 3 skeins each in colors 10153 Brown (A) and 10396 Rust (B), **5** bulky

- Size U.S. 13 (9mm) 40" (100cm) circular needle, or size needed to obtain gauge
- Blunt-tip yarn needle

### Gauge
19 stitches and 19 rows = 4" (10cm) in pattern
To save time, take time to check gauge.

## Note

For details on this stitch see page 86.

## Scarf

With A, loosely cast on 427 stitches.

ROW 1 (AND ALL ODD ROWS):
*Ssk, dropping only the first stitch off the left needle; repeat from * across, k1.

ROW 2 (AND ALL EVEN ROWS):
With B, *p2tog, dropping only the first stitch off the left needle; repeat from * across, p1.

Repeat Rows 1 and 2, changing color every other row (carry the unused yarn up the side as you go—no need to cut the yarn every time) until 33 rows have been worked, ending with A.

Bind off loosely in pattern.

## Finishing

Weave in all ends. Block piece lightly to the finished measurements if the edges curl.

MAKE IT MORE FEMININE

If browns aren't your bag, brighten this scarf up with colors Burgundy 10402 and Rose 10397.

# KNITTING
# WITH **SCISSORS**

I've never understood why knitters are so afraid of scissors. True, thrown willy-nilly into a knitting bag they can wreak havoc with a work in progress. But truth be told, they're the most useful tool in our knitting arsenal—capable of trimming yarn and making pom-poms of course, but when it comes to fixing mistakes, scissors can be more empowering than digital row counters and more time-saving than electric yarn winders.

I never go anywhere without scissors in my knitting bag, so flying during the post-9/11 airport security crackdown became a challenge. Like many knitters, I left my scissors at home and only traveled with yarns that could be broken by hand. Cotton and nylon were out, since the tensile strength of some of these fibers is strong enough that they could tow the plane from the gate. Projects on planes became simpler, as steeking at 30,000 feet was now out of the question.

Luckily the rules have changed, restrictions have been lightened, and you can now bring scissors onboard that are shorter than 4" (10cm) from the fulcrum. Unfortunately not all TSA officers are up-to-date on the rules, which I discovered on a recent flight from Hartford to San Francisco.

"Do you have a weapon in this bag?" asked the TSA officer.

"No, just a pair of scissors," I replied. It was an early-morning flight, and he was not amused.

"Step to the side," he said.

I obliged and took out my iPhone to look up the latest TSA travel restrictions while he ransacked my knitting bag looking for my own little WMD.

"Isn't this the latest information?" I said, handing the officer my phone. He reluctantly read it and called for his supervisor. While I was right about the scissors, it took four TSA officers, all taking turns measuring my scissors down to the micron, to make sure they were under the 4" (10cm) limit before they let me through. I gathered my bags—dignity a little bruised but the work-in-progress unharmed—and headed for my gate with only fifteen minutes left before boarding.

I took a seat next to a lovely but tired-looking woman who was just putting away her own knitting. Her name was Dottie, and she told me she was up all night knitting a sweater for her grandson, whom she was going to visit on the West Coast. She had adapted it from an adult pattern and made it shorter and narrower.

While cutting down a pattern from an adult size 48 to a 42 is easy, changing a pattern from an adult size to a child size isn't so simple. Our body proportions change as we grow from babies to children and again as we grow into adulthood. For one thing, arms get longer in proportion to our bodies. So Dottie had some problems. She showed me the sweater and how the sleeves (knit in the round) were about two inches too long for this eight-year-old's sweater. While she really needed to sleep, her plan was to spend the next six hours removing the sleeves from the body, unraveling them, reknitting and reattaching them—an ambitious task to accomplish in a cross-country flight, even for the most seasoned knitter.

"Is there a faster way to do this?" she asked.

"Sure," I said, pulling out the scissors that nearly closed down the airport not five minutes earlier.

Dottie handed me the sweater.

"Thanks for getting me started," she said, "undoing seams is always so hard for me."

With that, I proceeded to simply cut off the offending two inches of sleeve hanging at the bottom of the right sleeve.

"What—!" was all Dottie managed to scream before shock overcame her. People turned to see what was going on.

"I was just cutting off her arms," I told them, then imagined my explanation wouldn't fly so well with the security folks I had just tangled with.

"Breathe, relax," I told Dottie and our lookers-on. "It's all under control."

By cutting away the excess in a straight row, I exposed a round of live stitches that Dottie was able to slide onto her double-pointed needles and bind off at the new and proper length, all before we had even boarded the flight.

Cutting your knitting with scissors is a rite of passage all knitters need to experience. It ensures your dominance over the yarn. It keeps you in charge of your knitting. And it takes all the fear out of making mistakes, many of which can be fixed with a little snip.

On board, the flight attendant came by my seat after we reached our cruising altitude and brought me a glass of white wine.

"It's a gift from Dottie in seat 23F," she said.

"It's only 9:00 am," I said, but she only winked and went back to her duties.

Later that morning, I walked down the aisle to thank Dottie for her gift. I understood why she didn't wait until lunch service to send me the wine. There she was in 23F, sound asleep with that sweater, surely the softest pillow on the plane, tucked behind her neck.

# Chapter 4

# COLOR

Color is a dangerous subject when it comes to men's designs. Pink, yellow, and powder blue just aren't colors most men are going to covet. Across the board a successful boyfriend sweater is darker, muted, and monochromatic. Navy, gray, black, and deep red are always a good choice whether you're making these intarsia and Fair Isle creations for him or for yourself.

# INTARSIA

Intarsia allows you to create large colorful images in your knitting without carrying multiple strands of yarn across each row. When you get to the place where you need to change color, you drop one ball of yarn and pick up another. Imagine knitting a white sweater with a large blue square in the middle of the front. You'll begin to knit in white, when the blue square begins, you'll drop the white ball of yarn and pick up a ball of blue yarn. When you reach the end of the blue square, you'll drop the blue yarn and pick up another new ball of white yarn—that's three balls of yarn going at once. If your sections of color aren't very large, say 2" (5cm) diamonds or small polka dots, then entire balls of yarn will be too cumbersome. Instead, wind a small amount of yarn around a plastic bobbin or butterfly, which you can find at your local yarn store. This bobbin becomes your mini ball of yarn and will only be used for one particular diamond or polka dot as you get to it. You might have as many as ten bobbins hanging on the back of your garment as you knit, each allowing you to use a different color when you need it.

When you're ready to add new yarn or switch between yarns, here's what you do.

### Adding New Yarn

Place the new ball of yarn on the wrong side of your fabric, letting the front-end tail hang over onto the right side, between the needles. Pull the old previous ball (or bobbin) of yarn under and up over the new yarn, wrapping it counterclockwise, so it hangs down on the left side of the new yarn. Now

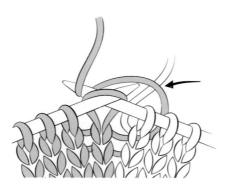

begin knitting or purling. The new tail is exposed, but later you'll pull it through to the wrong side, and weave it in to hide it.

### Going Back and Forth Between Yarns

When you reach your new color, drop the first yarn you're working with. Pick up the second ball of yarn and wrap it under and around the first yarn counterclockwise like you did when you added new yarn. Now you're ready to knit or purl, as the pattern indicates.

# DUPLICATE STITCH
## EMBROIDERY

This technique allows you to add a touch of color here and there, a single stitch or a single line (vertical, horizontal, or diagonal) without having to strand yarn or hang bobbins. After you've finished knitting your piece, thread a yarn needle with your new color and duplicate a knit stitch so that the new color covers an existing stitch. Here's how.

1. Place your threaded yarn needle at the back of your work and insert it from back to front through the center (between the legs of the V) of the stitch below the one you want to duplicate.

2. Insert the needle from right to left under the entire stitch (both legs of the V) above the one you are trying to duplicate, so that the needle seems to lift up that stitch and sticks back out on the left side.

3. Bring the needle down and insert it from front to back into the middle (between the legs of the V) of the same stitch where you started.

## THE SPIT SPLICE

Here's a great way to join new yarn without any knots or weaving in ends—but it only works on wool and blends that have at least 50 percent animal fibers. Fray the ends of the old and new yarns with your fingertips then intermingle the fibers, overlapping them about ½". Place the joined ends in your mouth (yeah, your mouth) and wet them with saliva. Now rub them together fast and hard between your palms to generate friction and heat. You will, in essence, be felting the ends together, creating a knotless join. One caveat: Don't try this with white, yellow, or other light-colored yarns. The color may darken a bit at the join and could be visible. This is best reserved for coarse yarns and darker colors.

You have re-created the movement of the knit yarn, covering the old stitch with a new color. Repeat this movement for any other stitches you would like to cover in a new color.

# FAIR ISLE OR
## STRANDED KNITTING

Fair Isle knitting is like the quadruple Lutz of the craft world—it's hard to do, but once it's in your repertoire your knitting will be on a world-class level. To accomplish this feat, you carry two yarns (each a different color) across each row working only one color at a time, with as many as 5 stitches in a row before switching colors. While it's tempting to allow the color not being used to simply hang back and wait until you need to pick it up, it's important to hold both strands throughout the process to ensure that the tension on each is relatively the same.

Some knitters hold one color in each hand, working the yarn in their right hand in the English (or sometimes called American) knitting style, while the yarn in their left hand is worked Continental style. Unless you're proficient in both styles, it's best to hold both strands in the hand you normally hold yarn in for single color knitting.

Once you pick a hand, there's another choice to make.

1. Hold both strands of yarn over your index finger.

2. Keep one strand over your index finger and the other over your middle finger. The only rule is to keep both strands in the same position throughout your entire project. Where the yarns lie on your fingers will have an impact on the tension. Changing the yarn's position will alter the look of your garment halfway through it.

It's rare that you will start your stranded knitting on the very first row of a garment. So don't worry about any special cast-on technique. Cast on in your preferred method unless the pattern specifically calls for a particular style.

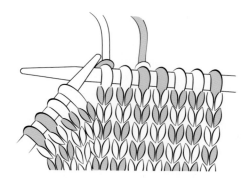

# **Varsity** Sweater

This may be the original boyfriend sweater—his school letter emblazoned in the middle of a cashmere blend pullover. The letter is knit in a slightly haloed alpaca so it stands out against the flat background, and it's created with an intarsia technique. Make one for yourself with his initial and make one for him with yours.

**Skill Level** ▶ Intermediate

## Finished Measurements

| Woman's Size | Man's Size | Bust/Chest | Length |
|---|---|---|---|
| S | XS | 39" (99cm) | 23¼" (59cm) |
| M | S | 42½" (108cm) | 23¾" (60.5cm) |
| L | M | 47" (119.5cm) | 24¼" (61.5cm) |
| XL | L | 50½" (128.5cm) | 24¾" (63cm) |
| XXL | XL | 55" (140cm) | 25¼" (64cm) |

If only one number is used, it applies to all sizes.

## Materials
- Cascade Yarns Cash Vero Aran (55% extra fine merino wool, 33% microfiber acrylic, 12% cashmere, each approximately 1¾ oz [50g] and 98 yd [90m], 10 (11, 12, 13, 15) balls in color 22 Taupe (A), (4) medium
- Berroco Ultra Alpaca (50% alpaca, 50% wool, each approximately 3½ oz [100g] and 215 yd [198m], 1 skein in color 6279 Potting Soil Mix (B), (4) medium
- One pair size U.S. 8 (5mm) needles, or size needed to obtain gauge
- Size U.S. 8 (5mm) 16" (40cm) circular needle
- Stitch markers
- Blunt-tip yarn needle

## Gauge
18 stitches and 24 rows = 4" (10cm) in stockinette stitch with A
To save time, take time to check gauge.

## Stitch Patterns
**Rib Pattern** *(even number of stitches)*
ROW 1 (RS): *K1, p1; repeat from * to end.
Repeat Row 1 for the pattern.

**Stockinette Stitch** *(any number of stitches)*
ROW 1 (RS): Knit across.
ROW 2: Purl across.
Repeat Rows 1 and 2 for pattern.

## Note
Divide B (contrast color for the letter) into 2 wound balls. Hold two strands together when working from the varsity letter chart; continue working with only one strand of A (main color) on each side of the varsity letter.

## Back

With the straight needles and A, cast on 88 (96, 106, 114, 124) stitches.

Work in the rib pattern until the piece measures 2" (5cm), ending with a wrong-side row.

Begin stockinette stitch and work even until the piece measures 13 (13½, 13½, 14, 14)" (33[34.5, 34.5, 35.5, 35.5]cm) from the cast-on edge, ending with a wrong-side row.

### SHAPE ARMHOLES
Bind off 4 (5, 6, 7, 8) stitches at the beginning of the next 2 rows; bind off 3 stitches at the beginning of the next 2 (2, 2, 2, 2) rows; bind off 2 stitches at the beginning of the next 0 (0, 2, 2, 4) rows—74 (80, 84, 90, 94) stitches remain.

Decrease 1 stitch on each side of every right-side row 3 (4, 4, 5, 5) times—68 (72, 76, 80, 84) stitches remain.

Work even until the armhole measures 9½ (9½, 10, 10, 10½)" (24 [24, 25.5, 25.5, 26.5]cm).

### SHAPE SHOULDERS
Bind off 10 (10, 11, 11, 12) stitches at the beginning of the next 2 rows; bind off 9 (10, 11, 11, 12) stitches at the beginning of the next 2 rows; bind off the remaining 30 (32, 32, 36, 36) stitches.

## Front

Work the same as the Back until the piece measures 6½ (7, 7, 7½, 7½)" (16.5 [18, 18, 19, 19] cm) from the cast-on edge, ending with a wrong-side row.

Mark the center of the row. Place markers out from the center marker for each side of the varsity letter pattern you choose to knit. For example, the letter used for the sample garment is 36 stitches wide, so a marker is placed 18 stitches out from both sides of the center marker; the center marker may be removed.

NEXT ROW (RS): With A, knit to the first marker, work the letter chart between markers, joining 2 strands of B to begin the letter, then joining a second ball of A, knit to the end.

NEXT ROW: With A, purl to the first marker, work the letter chart between markers, twisting yarns when changing colors, then with A purl to the end.

Continue in the pattern as established until the chart is complete and *at the same time,* shape the armholes the same as for the Back when the piece measures 13 (13½, 13½, 14, 14)" (33 [34.5, 34.5, 35.5, 35.5]cm) from the cast-on edge.

Work even until the armhole measures 7½ (7¼, 7¾, 7½, 8)" (19 [18.5, 19.5, 19, 20.5]cm), ending with a wrong-side row.

## SHAPE NECK

NEXT ROW (RS): Knit 26 (27, 29, 30, 32) stitches, join a second ball of A, bind off 16 (18, 18, 20, 20) stitches for neck, then knit the remaining 26 (27, 29, 30, 32) stitches.

Work both sides at once with separate balls of yarn and bind off 2 stitches at each neck edge twice—22 (23, 25, 26, 28) stitches remain on each side.

Decrease 1 stitch at each neck edge every other row 3 (3, 3, 4, 4) times—19 (20, 22, 22, 24) stitches remain.

Work even until the armhole measures the same as the back to the shoulders, ending with a wrong-side row.

## SHAPE SHOULDERS

Work the same as for the Back.

## Sleeves (Make 2)

With the straight needles and A, cast on 40 (42, 44, 46, 48) stitches.

Work in the rib pattern until the piece measures 2" (5cm), ending with a wrong-side row.

Begin stockinette stitch and increase 1 stitch at each side of every 4 rows 9 (12, 14, 16, 18) times, then every 6 rows 8 (6, 5, 4, 3) times—74 (78, 82, 86, 90) stitches.

Work even until the piece measures 17 (17, 17½, 17½, 18)" (43 [43, 44.5, 44.5, 45.5]cm) from the cast-on edge, ending with a wrong-side row.

## SHAPE CAP

Bind off 4 (5, 6, 7, 8) stitches at the beginning of the next 2 rows; bind off 3 stitches at the beginning of the next 2 (2, 2, 2, 2) rows; bind off 2 stitches at the beginning of the next 0 (0, 2, 2, 4) rows—60 (62, 60, 62, 60) stitches remain.

Decrease 1 stitch at each side of every right-side row 14 (15, 14, 16, 15) times—32 (32, 32, 30, 30) stitches remain.

Bind off 2 stitches at the beginning of the next 2 rows; bind off 4 (4, 4, 3, 3) stitches at the beginning of the next 2 rows.

Bind off the remaining 20 stitches.

## Finishing

Weave in all ends. Block all pieces to the finished measurements.

Sew the shoulder seams.

## Neckband

With the right side facing, using the circular needle and A, and beginning at the left shoulder, pick up and knit 17 (18, 18, 19, 19) stitches along the left neck edge, 17 (19, 19, 21, 21) stitches along the center front neck, 17 (18, 18, 19, 19) stitches along the right neck edge, and 31 (33, 33, 37, 37) stitches along the back neck—82 (88, 88, 96, 96) stitches. Place a marker for the beginning of the round, and join.

Work in the rib pattern for 1" (2.5cm). Bind off loosely in pattern.

Set in the Sleeves.

Sew the sleeve and side seams.

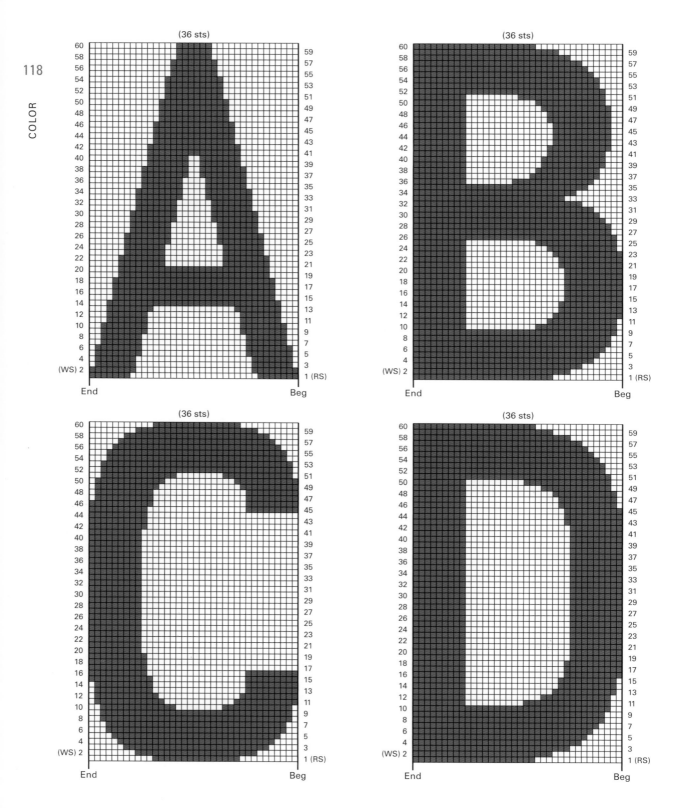

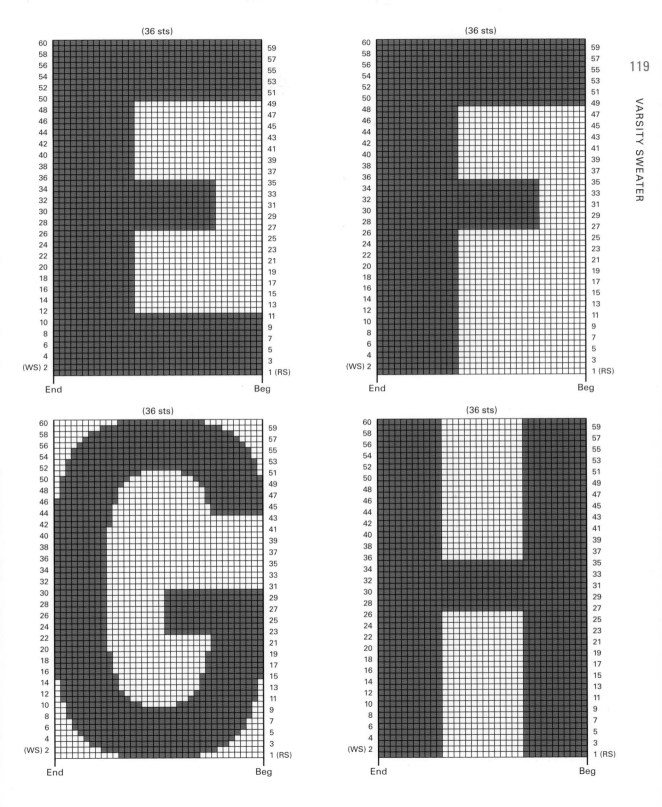

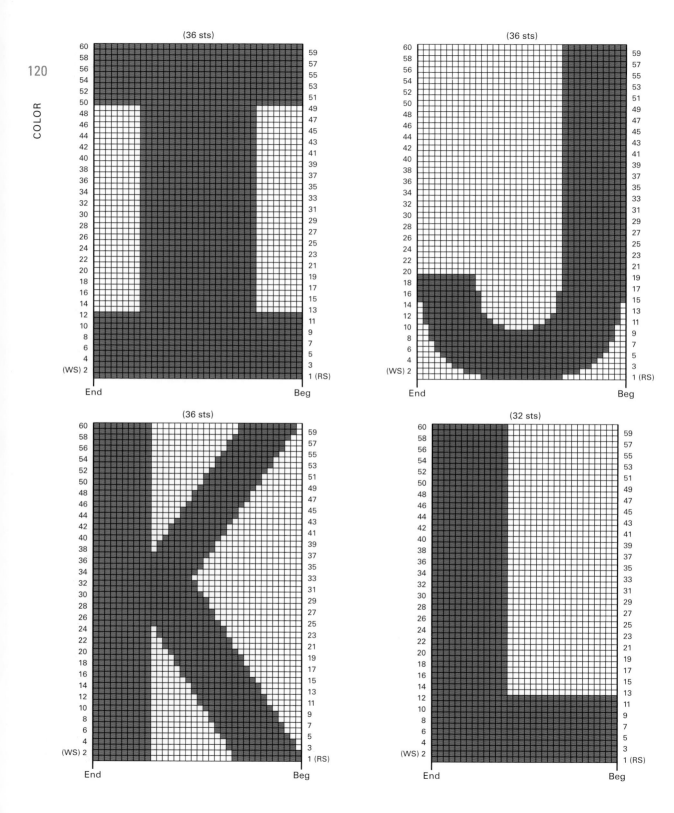

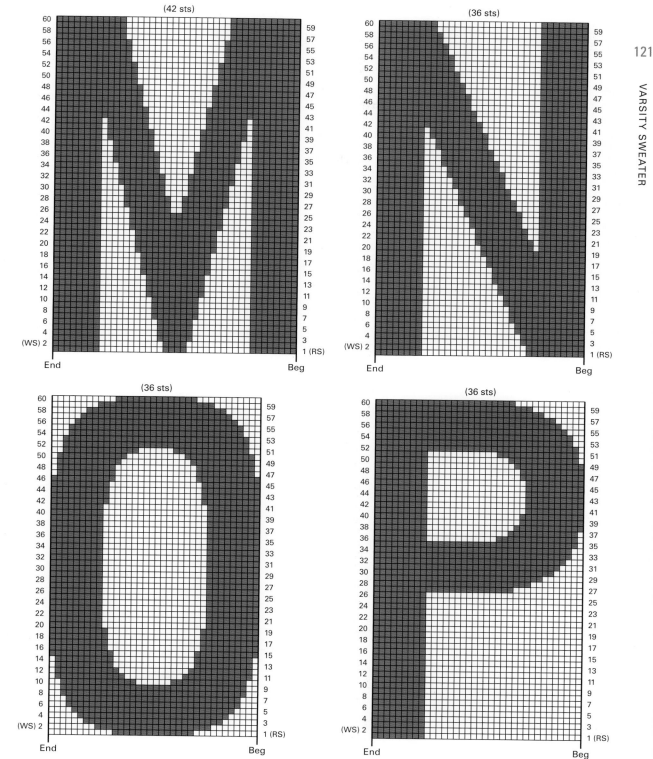

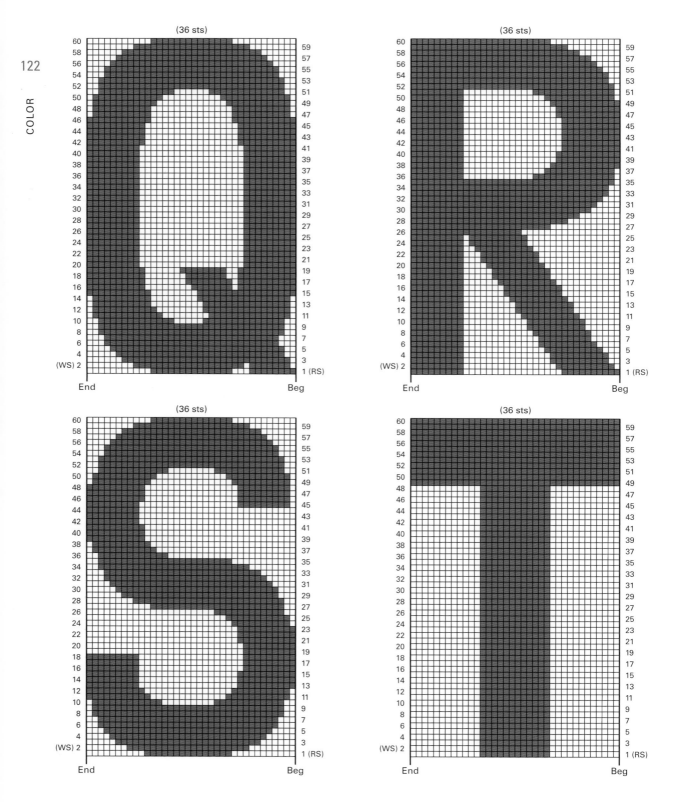

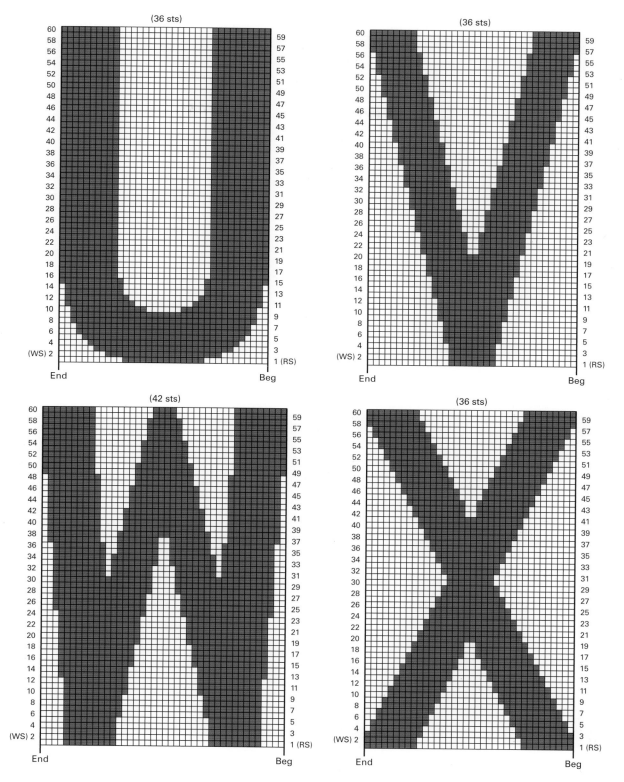

COLOR

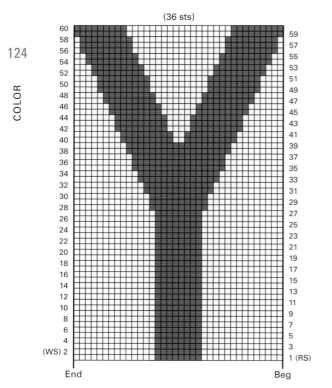

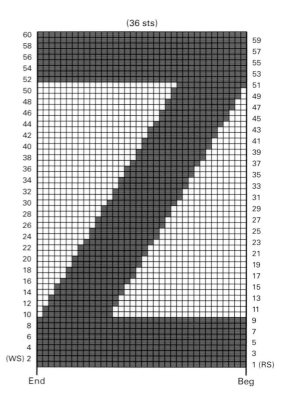

**STITCH KEY**

☐ = A

■ = B

# Funnel Neck Pullover
# with Raglan Details

This sweater has an extra wide funnel neck that isn't constraining so it will appeal to the guy who refuses to wear a turtleneck. The raglan seam is highlighted with contrasting yarn using duplicate stitch embroidery—a very handy color technique to have in your repertoire. Note that this sweater is oversized, so pay close attention to finished dimensions in case you want to make it more fitted.

**Skill Level** Easy

## Finished Measurements

| Woman's Size | Man's Size | Bust/Chest | Length |
|---|---|---|---|
| M | S | 43" (106.5cm) | 24½" (62cm) |
| L | M | 46½" (116cm) | 24¾" (63, cm) |
| XL | L | 50½" (125cm) | 25¾" (65.5cm) |
| XXL | XL | 54" (134.5cm) | 26¼" (66.5cm) |
| XXXL | XXL | 58½" (144cm) | 27¼" (69cm) |
| XXXXL | XXXL | 62" (155.5cm) | 27½" (70cm) |

If only one number is used, it applies to all sizes.

## Materials
• Berroco Blackstone Tweed (65% wool, 25% superkid mohair, 10% angora rabbit hair, each approximately 1¾ oz [50g] and 130 yd [119m], 9 (9, 10, 11, 12, 13) balls in color 2607 Wintry Mix (A) and 1 ball in 2601 Clover Honey (B), **4** medium
• One pair size U.S. 7 (4.5mm) knitting needles, or size needed to obtain gauge
• Blunt-tip yarn needle

## Gauge
17½ stitches and 26 rows = 4" (10cm) in stockinette stitch; 19 stitches and 26 rows = 4" (10cm) in sleeve rib pattern
To save time, take time to check gauge.

## Stitch Pattern
Sleeve Rib *(multiple of 6 stitches)*
ROW 1 (RS): K5, *p2, k4; repeat from * to the last stitch, k1.
ROW 2: P5, *k2, p4; repeat from * to the last stitch, p1.
Repeat Rows 1 and 2 for the pattern.

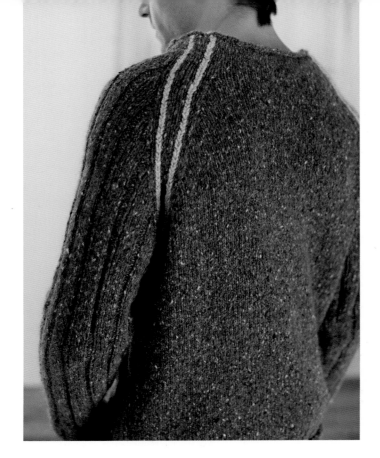

## Front

Work the same as the Back.

## Sleeves (Make 2)

With Color A, cast on 48 (48, 54, 54, 60, 60) stitches.

Work in the sleeve rib pattern for 2" (5cm), ending with a wrong-side row.

**NEXT ROW (RS):** K5, kfb, work in pattern to the last 5 stitches, kfb, k5—50 (50, 56, 56, 62, 62) stitches.

Repeat the increase row every 6 rows 2 (6, 2, 14, 10, 18) times, then every 8 rows 10 (8, 11, 2, 5, 0) times—74 (78, 82, 88, 92, 98) stitches. Work the new stitches into the rib pattern while maintaining the 5 stockinette stitches on each end.

Work even until the piece measures 17½ (18, 18½, 18½, 19, 19)" (44.5 [45.5, 47, 47, 48.5, 48.5]cm) from the cast-on edge, ending with a wrong-side row.

### SHAPE CAP

Bind off 2 (3, 4, 5, 6, 8) stitches at the beginning of the next 2 rows—70 (72, 74, 78, 80, 82) stitches remain.

**NEXT ROW (RS):** K5, ssk, knit to the last 7 stitches, k2tog, k5—68 (70, 72, 76, 78, 80) stitches remain.

Repeat the decrease row every right-side row 24 (26, 27, 29, 30, 32) times more—20 (18, 18, 18, 18, 16) stitches remain.

Work even for 2¾" (7cm). Bind off the remaining stitches.

## Back

With A, cast on 94 (102, 110, 118, 126, 136) stitches.

Work in stockinette stitch until piece measures 14½ (14½, 15, 15, 15½, 15½)" (37 [37, 38, 38, 39.5, 39.5]cm) from the cast-on edge, ending with a wrong-side row.

### SHAPE ARMHOLES

Bind off 2 (3, 4, 5, 6, 8) stitches at the beginning of the next 2 rows—90 (96, 102, 108, 114, 120) stitches remain.

**NEXT ROW (RS):** K5, sssk, knit to the last 8 stitches, k3tog, k5—86 (92, 98, 104, 110, 116) stitches remain.

Repeat double decrease row every right-side row 0 (0, 0, 0, 1, 2) more time(s)—86 (92, 98, 104, 106, 108) stitches.

Work 1 row even.

**NEXT ROW (RS):** K5, ssk, knit to the last 7 stitches, k2tog, k5. Repeat the decrease row every right-side row 23 (25, 26, 28, 28, 29) more times—38 (40, 44, 46, 48, 48) stitches remain.

Work even for 2¾" (7cm). Bind off the remaining stitches.

## Finishing

Weave in all ends. Block all pieces before assembling, blocking sleeves so ribs lie flat and open.

Sew the Sleeves to the Front and Back along the raglan armhole edges. Sew the side and sleeve seams.

With the blunt-tip needle and B use the duplicate stitch technique (page 112) to add one line of the contrast color on each side of all raglan armhole seams from the armhole to the neck edge. Work the duplicate stitch one stitch in from each seam.

## FUNNEL NECK PULLOVER WITH RAGLAN DETAILS **SCHEMATIC**

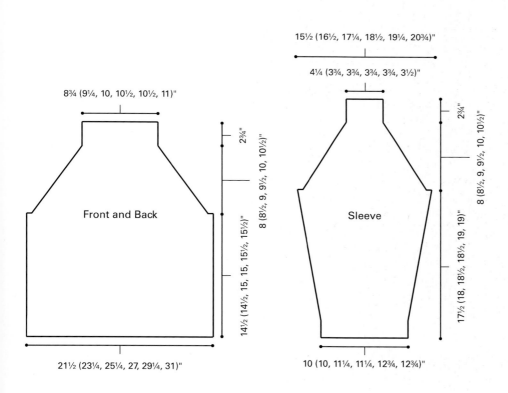

Front and Back

8¾ (9¼, 10, 10½, 10½, 11)"

2¾"

8 (8½, 9, 9½, 10, 10½)"

14½ (14½, 15, 15, 15½, 15½)"

21½ (23¼, 25¼, 27, 29¼, 31)"

Sleeve

15½ (16½, 17¼, 18½, 19¼, 20¾)"

4¼ (3¾, 3¾, 3¾, 3¾, 3½)"

2¾"

8 (8½, 9, 9½, 10, 10½)"

17½ (18, 18½, 18½, 19, 19)"

10 (10, 11¼, 11¼, 12¾, 12¾)"

# Fair Isle Cardigan

Here's a distinctly Southwest design in a subtle big-city color palette. Although it's designed to be knit using the stranded colorwork technique, it's easy to adapt to intarsia if that's your preferred method of changing color. Either way, duplicate stitch embroidery creates the final touch.

**Skill Level** ▶ Advanced

## Finished Measurements

| Woman's Size | Man's Size | Bust/Chest | Length |
|---|---|---|---|
| S | XS | 38¼" (97cm) | 26¾" (68cm) |
| M | S | 42¼" (107.5cm) | 27¼" (69cm) |
| L | M | 46¼" (117.5cm) | 28" (71cm) |
| XL | L | 50¼" (127.5cm) | 28½" (72cm) |
| XXL | XL | 54¼" (138cm) | 29" (74cm) |
| XXXL | XXL | 58¼" (148cm) | 29¾" (75.5cm) |

If only one number is used, it applies to all sizes.

## Materials
- Zitron Gobi (40% extra fine merino wool, 30% camel, 30% alpaca, each approximately 1¾ oz [50g] and 87 yards [79m]; 9 (11, 12, 13, 14, 15) balls in color 02 Black (A), 3 (4, 4, 5, 5, 6) balls in color 12 Vanilla (B), and 2 (3, 3, 3, 4, 4) balls in color 10 Blue/Gray (C), 〔4〕 medium
- One pair size U.S. 8 (5mm) needles, or size needed to obtain gauge
- Size U.S. 8 (5mm) 36" (91cm) circular needles
- Blunt-tip yarn needle
- 9 buttons 1" (25mm) wide

## Gauge
16 stitches and 22 rows = 4" (10cm) in stockinette stitch
To save time, take time to check gauge.

## Stitch Patterns
**K1, P1 Rib** *(multiple of 2 stitches)*
ROW 1: *K1, p1; repeat from * to the end.
Repeat Row 1 for the first rib pattern.

**K1, P1 Rib** *(multiple of 2 + 1 stitches)*
ROW 1: K1, *p1, k1; repeat from * to the end.
ROW 2: P1, *k1, p1; repeat from * to the end.
Repeat Rows 1 and 2 for the second rib pattern.

## Notes
The pattern charts should end at the armhole/underarm for all sizes. Any adjustment to length should be done in the plain section below the charts only.

## Back

With A and the straight needles, cast on 80 (88, 96, 104, 112, 120) stitches.

Work in the first rib pattern until the piece measures 1¾" (4.5cm), ending with a wrong-side row.

Change to stockinette stitch and work 4 (6, 6, 6, 8, 8) rows.

Work the back chart for your size through row 74 of the chart.

Change to A and work 2 rows of stockinette stitch, ending with a wrong-side row. The piece should measure 16½ (16¾, 16¾, 16¾, 17, 17)" (42 [42.5, 42.5, 42.5, 43, 43]cm) from the cast-on edge.

### SHAPE ARMHOLES

Bind off 4 (5, 6, 7, 8, 9) stitches at the beginning of the next 2 rows—72 (78, 84, 90, 96, 102) stitches remain.

DECREASE ROW (RS): K1, k2tog, knit to the last 3 sts, k2tog tbl, k1—70 (76, 82, 88, 94, 100) stitches remain.

Repeat the decrease row every right-side row 24 (25, 27, 28, 29, 31) times more—22 (26, 28, 32, 36, 38) stitches remain. Bind off the remaining stitches.

## Right Front

With A and the straight needles, cast on 37 (41, 45, 49, 53, 57) stitches.

Work in the second rib pattern until the piece measures 1¾" (4.5cm), ending with a wrong-side row.

Change to stockinette stitch and work 4 (6, 6, 6, 8, 8) rows.

Work the right front chart for your size through row 74 of the chart.

Change to A and work 3 rows of stockinette stitch, ending with a right-side row. The piece should measure about 16½ (16¾, 16¾, 16¾, 17, 17)" (42 [42.5, 42.5, 42.5, 43, 43]cm) from the cast-on edge.

### SHAPE ARMHOLE

NEXT ROW (WS): Bind off 4 (5, 6, 7, 8, 9) stitches, then purl to the end—33 (36, 39, 42, 45, 48) stitches remain.

DECREASE ROW (RS): Knit to the last 3 stitches, k2tog tbl, k1—32 (35, 38, 41, 44, 47) stitches remain.

Repeat the decrease row every right-side row 21 (22, 22, 23, 24, 24) times more—11 (13, 16, 18, 20, 23) stitches remain, ending with a wrong-side row.

### SHAPE NECK

Decrease 1 stitch at the neck edge every row 6 (7, 9, 10, 12, 14) times. *At the same time,* continue the raglan decreases on every right-side row 3 (4, 5, 6, 6, 7) times—2 stitches remain.

Cut the yarn and pull the tail through the remaining stitches to fasten off.

## Left Front

With A and the straight needles, cast on 37 (41, 45, 49, 53, 57) stitches.

Work in the second rib pattern until the piece measures 1¾" (4.5cm) ending with a wrong-side row.

Change to stockinette stitch and work 4 (6, 6, 6, 8, 8) rows.

Work the left front chart for your size through row 74 of the chart.

Change to A and work 2 rows of stockinette stitch, ending with a wrong-side row. The piece should measure about 16½ (16¾, 16¾, 16¾, 17, 17)" (42 [42.5, 42.5, 42.5, 43, 43]cm) from the cast-on edge.

### SHAPE ARMHOLE

NEXT ROW (RS): Bind off 4 (5, 6, 7, 8, 9) stitches, then knit to the end—33 (36, 39, 42, 45, 48) stitches remain.

NEXT ROW (WS): Purl to the last 3 stitches, p2tog, p1—32 (35, 38, 41, 44, 47) stitches remain.

Repeat the decrease row every wrong-side row 21 (22, 22, 23, 24, 24) times more—11 (13, 16, 18, 20, 23) stitches remain, ending with a right-side row.

### SHAPE NECK

Decrease 1 stitch at the neck edge every row 6 (7, 9, 10, 12, 14) times. *At the same time,* continue the raglan decreases every wrong-side row 3 (4, 5, 6, 6, 7) times—2 stitches remain.

Cut the yarn and pull the tail through the remaining stitches to fasten off.

## Sleeves (Make 2)

With A and the straight needles, cast on 41 (43, 45, 47, 49, 51) sts.

Work in the second rib pattern until the piece measures 2 (2¼, 2¼, 2¼, 2¼, 2½)" (5 [5.5, 5.5, 5.5, 5.5, 6.5]cm), ending with a wrong-side row.

Repeat the decrease row every right-side 22 (23, 25, 26, 27, 29) times more—7 stitches remain.

Work 5 rows even. Bind off the remaining stitches.

## Finishing

With the blunt-tip yarn needle and A, use the duplicate stitch technique (page 112) to add the centers of the small diamonds on both Front pieces, the Back and the Sleeves, referring to the charts.

Weave in all the ends. Block all pieces to the finished measurements.

Sew the raglan seams. Sew the side and sleeve seams.

## Collar

With the circular needle, A, and the right side facing, pick up and knit 50 (56, 64, 70, 80, 86) stitches along the neck edge.

Work back and forth in the first rib pattern for 2" (5cm). Bind off all stitches in pattern.

## Buttonhole Band

With the circular needle, A, and the right side facing, begin at the top of the collar, pick up and knit 135 (139, 139, 141, 143, 143) stitches along the left front edge to the bottom edge.

**NEXT ROW (WS):** P1, *k1, p1; repeat from * to the end.

Work 3 rows more of rib as established.

**NEXT ROW (WS):** *P1, k2tog, (yo) twice, (k1, p1) 6 times, k1, p2tog,

Change to stockinette stitch and work until the piece measures about 4¾ (5¼, 5¼, 5½, 5½, 5¾)" (12 [13.5, 13.5, 14, 14, 14.5]cm) from the cast-on edge, ending, with a right-side row.

**NEXT ROW (WS):** P1, pfb, purl to the last stitch, pfb, p1—43 (45, 47, 49, 51, 53) stitches.

Work the sleeve chart for your size and continue increasing at each end every 4 rows 0 (0, 0, 3, 7, 12) times, every 6 rows 0 (5, 12, 10, 7, 4) times, then every 8 rows 9 (5, 0, 0, 0, 0) times—61 (65, 71, 75, 79, 85) stitches. Work the new stitches into the pattern as shown on the chart.

When the chart is complete, the piece should measure 18½ (19, 19, 19¼, 19¼, 19½)" (47 [48.5, 48.5, 49, 49, 49.5]cm) from the cast-on edge, ending with a wrong-side row.

Change to A and work 2 rows of stockinette stitch.

### SHAPE CAP
Bind off 4 (5, 6, 7, 8, 9) stitches at the beginning of the next 2 rows—53 (55, 59, 61, 63, 67) stitches remain.

**NEXT ROW (RS):** K1, k2tog, knit to the last 3 stitches, k2tog tbl, k1—51 (53, 57, 59, 61, 65) stitches remain.

(yo) twice, (p1, k1) 6 times; repeat from * 3 times more, p1, k2tog, (yo) twice, (k1, p1) to the end.

**NEXT ROW:** Work in the rib pattern, dropping the extra yarn over at each buttonhole, and working the enlarged yarn over into the rib pattern. Note, the double yarn over just created a larger buttonhole.

Work 2 rows even. Bind off all stitches in pattern.

## Button Band

With the circular needle, A, and the right side facing, begin at the bottom edge, pick up and knit 135 (139, 139, 141, 143, 143) stitches along the right front edge to the top of the collar.

**NEXT ROW (WS):** P1, *k1, p1; repeat from * to the end.

Work 6 rows more of rib as established, ending with a wrong-side row. Bind off all stitches in pattern.

Sew the buttons to the button band opposite the buttonholes.

## FAIR ISLE CARDIGAN **SCHEMATIC**

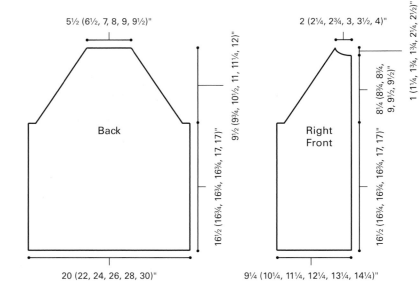

5½ (6½, 7, 8, 9, 9½)"

Back

9½ (9¾, 10½, 11, 11¼, 12)"

16½ (16¾, 16¾, 16¾, 17, 17)"

20 (22, 24, 26, 28, 30)"

2 (2¼, 2¾, 3, 3½, 4)"

Right Front

1 (1¼, 1¾, 1¾, 2¼, 2½)"

8¼ (8¾, 8¾, 9, 9½, 9½)"

16½ (16¾, 16¾, 16¾, 17, 17)"

9¼ (10¼, 11¼, 12¼, 13¼, 14¼)"

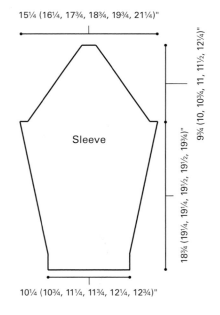

15¼ (16¼, 17¾, 18¾, 19¾, 21¼)"

Sleeve

9¾ (10, 10¾, 11, 11½, 12¼)"

18¾ (19¼, 19¼, 19½, 19½, 19¾)"

10¼ (10¾, 11¼, 11¾, 12¼, 12¾)"

## BACK
### (mult 16 sts)

End Woman's M (1X, 3X)
Man's S (L, 2X)

End Woman's S (L, 2X)
Man's XS (M, 1X)

16-stitch
repeat
work 5 (5, 6, 6, 7, 7)
times

Beg Woman's M (1X, 3X)
Man's S (L, 2X)

Beg Woman's S (L, 2X)
Man's XS (M, 1X)

**COLOR KEY**

 = A

☐ = B

 = C

**STITCH KEY**

☐ = K on RS; p on WS

⊠ = Work in B; add A using duplicate stitch

CONTINUES ➡

COLOR

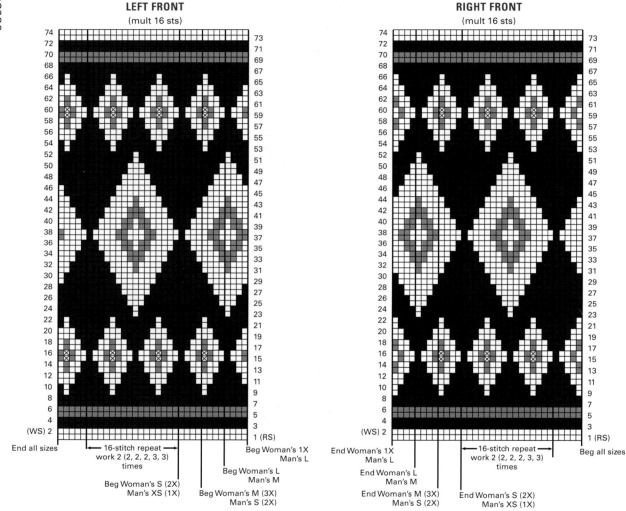

**LEFT FRONT**
(mult 16 sts)

**RIGHT FRONT**
(mult 16 sts)

## SLEEVE
(mult 16 sts)

16-stitch repeat
work 2 times

**COLOR KEY**

■ = A
□ = B
▨ = C

**STITCH KEY**

□ = K on RS; p on WS
⊠ = Work in B; add A using duplicate stitch

**SIZES FOR SLEEVE SHAPING**

— = Woman's size S/Man's size XS
— = Woman's size M/Man's size S
— = Woman's size L/Man's size M
— = Woman's size 1X/Man's size L
— = Woman's size 2X/Man's size 1X
— = Woman"s size 3X/Man's size 2X

# **Plaid** Pullover

Knitting plaid is easier than it looks. Two-color stranded technique makes up the bulk of the colorwork in this classic midcentury modern pullover. The third accent color is added after you've finished, using duplicate stitch embroidery. And the solid sleeves make this boyfriend sweater even easier to complete.

**Skill Level** ▸ Intermediate

**Finished Measurements**

| Woman's Size | Man's Size | Bust/Chest | Length |
|---|---|---|---|
| S | XS | 36" (91cm) | 25¼" (64cm) |
| M | S | 40½" (103cm) | 26" (66cm) |
| L | M | 44" (112cm) | 26¾" (68cm) |
| XL | L | 48" (122cm) | 27½" (70cm) |
| XXL | XL | 52" (132cm) | 28¼" (72cm) |
| XXXL | XXL | 56½" (143.5cm) | 29" (74cm) |

If only one number is used, it applies to all sizes.
Pictured in size Woman's Medium/Man's Small

**Materials**
- Berroco Vintage (50% acrylic, 40% wool, 10% nylon, each approximately 3½ oz [100g] and 217 yd [198m], 5 (5, 5, 7, 7, 8) skeins in color 5117 Chambray (A), 2 (2, 2, 3, 3, 3) skeins in color 5185 Tide Pool (B), and 1 (1, 1, 1, 1, 1) skein color 5194 Breezeway (C), ④ medium
- One pair size U.S. 7 (4.5mm) needles, or size needed to obtain gauge
- Size U.S. 7 (4.5mm) 16" (40cm) circular needle
- Stitch holders
- Blunt-tip yarn needle

**Gauge**
19 stitches and 26 rows = 4" (10cm) in stockinette stitch
19 stitches and 22 rows = 4" (10cm) in stockinette stitch in plaid pattern
To save time, take time to check gauge.

**Stitch Pattern**
Rib Pattern *(even number stitches)*
ROW 1 (WS): *K1, p1; repeat from * to end.
Repeat Row 1 for the pattern.

# Back

With the straight needles and A, cast on 88 (98, 106, 116, 126, 136) stitches.

Work in the rib pattern until the piece measures 2½" (6.5cm) from the cast-on edge, ending with a wrong-side row.

Change to stockinette stitch and work the plaid chart for your size until the piece measures 16 (16¼, 16½, 16¾, 17, 17¼)" (40.5 [41.5, 42, 42.5, 43, 44] cm) from the cast-on edge, ending with a wrong-side row.

### SHAPE ARMHOLES

Bind off 2 (3, 4, 5, 7, 8) stitches at the beginning of the next 2 rows—84 (92, 98, 106, 112, 120) stitches remain.

Decrease 1 stitch at each side of every right-side row 2 (2, 3, 4, 5, 7) times—80 (88, 92, 98, 102, 106) stitches remain.

Work even until armhole measures 8¼ (8¾, 9¼, 9¾, 10¼, 10¾)" (21 [22, 23.5, 25, 26, 27.5] cm), ending with a wrong-side row.

### SHAPE RIGHT SHOULDER AND NECK

Bind off 6 (7, 8, 8, 9, 8) sts, work 22 (25, 25, 28, 28, 31) sts, place the next 24 (24, 26, 26, 28, 28) stitches on a holder for the neck and the remaining 28 (32, 33, 36, 37, 39) stitches on a second holder for the left shoulder, turn.

Decrease 1 stitch at the neck edge every row 4 times and bind off 6 (7, 7, 8, 8, 9) stitches at the shoulder edge 3 times. Break yarn.

### SHAPE LEFT SHOULDER AND NECK

Return the 28 (32, 33, 36, 37, 39) stitches held for the left shoulder to the straight needles.

Join the yarn to begin with a wrong-side row. Continuing in the established pattern, bind off 6 (7, 8, 8, 9, 8) stitches, then work to the end of the row.

Decrease 1 stitch at the neck edge every row 4 times and bind off 6 (7, 7, 8, 8, 9) stitches at the shoulder edge 3 times.

# Front

Work the same as the Back until the armhole measures 3 (3½, 3½, 3½, 4, 4)" (7.5 [9, 9, 9, 10, 10]cm), ending with a wrong-side row.

### SHAPE LEFT NECK AND SHOULDER

NEXT ROW (RS): Work 38 (42, 44, 47, 49, 51) stitches, ssk, place the remaining 40 (44, 46, 49, 51, 53) stitches on a holder, turn.

Decrease 1 stitch at the neck edge every right-side row 15 (15, 16, 16, 17, 17) times and *at the same time,* when the armhole measures 8¼ (8¾, 9¼, 9¾, 10¼, 10¾)" (21 [22, 23.5, 25, 26, 27.5] cm) bind off at the shoulder edge 6 (7, 8, 8, 9, 8) stitches once, then 6 (7, 7, 8, 8, 9) stitches 3 times.

Break yarn.

### SHAPE RIGHT NECK AND SHOULDER

Place the remaining stitches on the straight needles. Join the yarn to begin with a right-side row.

NEXT ROW (RS): K2tog, work to the end of the row in the established pattern—39 (43, 45, 48, 50, 52) stitches. Continue decreasing 1 stitch at the neck edge every

right-side row 15 (15, 16, 16, 17, 17) times more and *at the same time,* when the armhole measures 8¼ (8¾, 9¼, 9¾, 10¼, 10¾)" (21 [22, 23.5, 25, 26, 27.5]), bind off at the shoulder edge 6 (7, 8, 8, 9, 8) stitches once, then 6 (7, 7, 8, 8, 9) stitches 3 times. Break yarn.

## Sleeves (Make 2)

With the straight needles and A, cast on 43 (45, 45, 47, 47, 49) stitches.

**ROW 1 (WS):** K1, *p1, k1; repeat from * to the end.

**ROW 2:** P1, *k1, p1; repeat from * to the end.

Work in the established rib pattern until piece measures 2" (5cm), ending with a wrong-side row.

Change to stockinette stitch and increase 1 stitch at each end of the first row—45 (47, 47, 49, 49, 51) stitches. Continue increasing every 2 rows 0 (0, 0, 0, 0, 3) times, every 4 rows 3 (6, 15, 18, 24, 24) times, then every 6 rows 15 (13, 7, 5, 1, 0) time(s)—81 (85, 91, 95, 99, 105) stitches. Work even until piece measures 18½" (47cm) from the cast-on edge, ending with a wrong-side row.

### SHAPE CAP

Bind off 3 (4, 5, 6, 7, 9) stitches at the beginning of the next 2 rows—75 (77, 81, 83, 85, 87) stitches. Decrease 1 stitch at each edge of every right-side row 10 (11, 12, 13, 14, 14) times, then every row 14 times. Bind off 3 stitches at the beginning of the next 4 rows. Bind off the remaining 15 (15, 17, 17, 17, 19) stitches.

## Finishing

With the blunt-tip yarn needle and C, use duplicate stitch embroidery (see p. 112) to add the vertical lines on the Front and Back pieces, referring to the chart.

Weave in all ends. Block all pieces to the finished measurements.

Sew the shoulder seams.

Sew the side and sleeve seams.

## Neckband

With the circular needle, A, and the right side facing, begin at the bottom of the front neck, pick up and knit 31 (33, 36, 38, 41, 43) stitches along the right front neck, 8 stitches along the right back neck edge, knit the 24 (24, 26, 26, 28, 28) stitches from the back neck holder, pick up and knit 8 stitches along the left back neck edge, and 31 (33, 36, 38, 41, 43) stitches down left front neck—102 (106, 114, 118, 126, 130) stitches.

Work back and forth in the rib pattern for 6 rows. Bind off all stitches in pattern.

Sew the ends of the neckband to the neck edges using the photos on pp. 138–139 as a guide.

Sew in the sleeves.

## MAKE IT MORE FEMININE

Plaids and tartans easily cross gender boundaries, but this sweater may be better fit for a woman when done up in reds and purples. Try colors 5181 Black Cherry = A, 5180 Dried Plum = B, and 5184 Sloe Berry = C.

COLOR

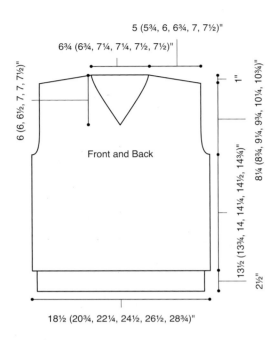

5 (5¾, 6, 6¾, 7, 7½)"

6¾ (6¾, 7¼, 7¼, 7½, 7½)"

6 (6, 6½, 7, 7, 7½)"

Front and Back

1"

8¼ (8¾, 9¼, 9¾, 10¼, 10¾)"

13½ (13¾, 14, 14¼, 14½, 14¾)"

2½"

18½ (20¾, 22¼, 24½, 26½, 28¾)"

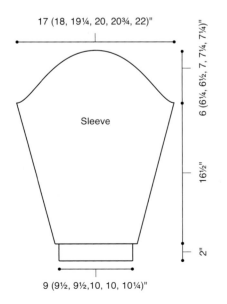

17 (18, 19¼, 20, 20¾, 22)"

Sleeve

6 (6¼, 6½, 7, 7¼, 7¼)"

16½"

2"

9 (9½, 9½, 10, 10, 10¼)"

## DUPLICATE STITCH TO THE RESCUE

Rescuing colorwork mistakes is easy with duplicate stitch embroidery. We've all misread a color chart at one point and know that frogging a piece of colorwork can be heartbreaking. But if your mistake is limited to a small section, a missed color here and there, a little duplicate stitch embroidery might just save the day. Simply use this technique to change the few miscolored stitches into their proper color—after the fact. Just think of it as knitting sleight-of-hand.

(mult 25 sts)

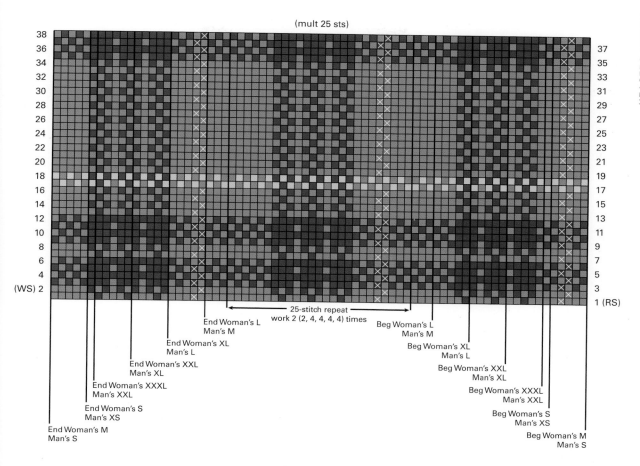

25-stitch repeat
work 2 (2, 4, 4, 4) times

End Woman's L
Man's M

End Woman's XL
Man's L

End Woman's XXL
Man's XL

End Woman's XXXL
Man's XXL

End Woman's S
Man's XS

End Woman's M
Man's S

Beg Woman's L
Man's M

Beg Woman's XL
Man's L

Beg Woman's XXL
Man's XL

Beg Woman's XXXL
Man's XXL

Beg Woman's S
Man's XS

Beg Woman's M
Man's S

**COLOR KEY**

■ = A

■ = B

■ = C

**STITCH KEY**

□ = K on RS; p on WS

⊠ = Work in A; add C using duplicate stitch

⊠ = Work in B; add C using duplicate stitch

# Houndstooth Cardigan

This contemporary houndstooth jacket pairs a classic pattern with a boxy semi–dropped shoulder for comfort and style. The yarn is a unique blend of merino, silk, and New Zealand possum. Unlike their northern cousins, these animals have a thick fur coat, which lends warmth and a soft halo to this sweater.

**Skill Level** ▷ Advanced

## Finished Measurements

| Woman's Size | Man's Size | Bust/Chest | Length |
|---|---|---|---|
| XXS | XS | 33¾" (85.5cm) | 25¼" (64cm) |
| XS | S | 39" (99cm) | 26" (66cm) |
| S | M | 44¼" (112.5cm) | 26¾" (68cm) |
| M/L | L | 50¾" (129cm) | 27½" (70cm) |
| XL/XXL | XL | 55" (139.5cm) | 28¼" (72cm) |

If only one number is used, it applies to all sizes.
Pictured in size Woman's XS/Man's Small

## Materials

- Supreme Possum Merino 8 Ply (50% merino, 40% possum fur, 10% silk, each approximately 1¾ oz [50g] and 131 yd [125m]), 9 (10, 11, 13, 14) balls in color A Natural (A) and 4 (5, 5, 6, 7) balls in color Black (B), ( 3 ) light
- One pair size U.S. 5 (3.75mm) needles, or size needed to obtain gauge
- Size U.S. 5 (3.75mm) 40" (100cm) circular needle
- Blunt-tip yarn needle
- Separating zipper 18 (18, 20, 20, 20)" (45.5 [45.5, 51, 51, 51]cm) long (for a man's sweater; optional for a woman)

## Gauge

24 stitches and 26 rows = 4" (10cm) in houndstooth pattern
To save time, take time to check gauge.

## Stitch Patterns

**Cuff Rib Pattern** (*multiple of 4 stitches + 2*)
**ROW 1 (RS):** K1, *k3, p1; repeat from * to last stitch, k1.
**ROW 2 (WS):** P1, *k1, p3; repeat from * to last stitch, p1.
Repeat rows 1 and 2 for the pattern.

**Zipper Band Rib Pattern** (*multiple of 2 stitches + 1*)
**ROW 1 (WS):** P1, *k1, p1; repeat from * to the end.
**ROW 2 (RS):** K1, *p1, k1; repeat from * to the end.
Repeat rows 1 and 2 for the pattern.

## Note

When sewing in the zipper, place the bottom at the cast-on edge and the top of the teeth where the front neck shaping begins. Fold any extra tape back toward the wrong side and tack down to hide it.

## Back

Have you measured your gauge in the houndstooth pattern? Great.

With A and the straight needles, cast on 100 (118, 134, 152, 170) stitches.

Work in the cuff rib pattern until the piece measures about 3½" (9cm) from the cast-on edge, ending with a right-side row.

NEXT ROW (WS): Work in rib and increase 2 (2, 4, 4, 4) stitches evenly spaced across the row—102 (120, 138, 156, 174) stitches.

Begin the houndstooth pattern and work even until piece measures 16¾ (17, 17¼, 17½, 17¾)" (42.5 [43, 44, 44.5, 45]cm) from the cast-on edge, ending with a wrong-side row.

### SHAPE ARMHOLES

Bind off 7 (12, 16, 21, 25) stitches at the beginning of the next 2 rows—88 (96, 106, 114, 124) stitches remain.

Work even until the armhole measures 8 (8½, 9, 9½, 10)" (20.5 [21.5, 23, 24, 25.5]cm), ending with a wrong-side row.

### SHAPE NECK

NEXT ROW (RS): Work in pattern across 22 (24, 29, 31, 36) stitches, join a second ball of B, bind off the center 44 (48, 48, 52, 52) stitches, join a second ball of A and work in pattern across

the remaining 22 (24, 29, 31, 36) stitches.

Work both sides at once with separate balls of yarn.

Work even in the pattern until the armhole measures 8½ (9, 9½, 10, 10½)" (21.5 [23, 24, 25.5, 26.5]cm). Bind off the remaining stitches.

## Right Front

With A and the straight needles, cast on 38 (46, 54, 62, 70) stitches.

Work in the cuff rib pattern until the piece measures about 3½" (9cm) from the cast-on edge, ending with a right-side row.

NEXT ROW (WS): Work in rib and increase 2 stitches evenly spaced across the row—40 (48, 56, 64, 72) stitches.

Begin the houndstooth pattern and work even until piece measures 16¾ (17, 17¼, 17½, 17¾)" (42.5 [43, 44, 44.5, 45]cm) from the cast-on edge, ending with a right-side row.

### SHAPE ARMHOLE

NEXT ROW (WS): Bind off 8 (12, 15, 19, 22) stitches, work in the pattern to the end of the row—32 (36, 41, 45, 50) stitches remain.

Work even until the armhole measures 1½" (3.8cm), ending with a wrong-side row.

### SHAPE NECK

DECREASE ROW (RS): K2tog, work in the pattern to the end of the row—31 (35, 40, 44, 49) stitches remain.

Repeat the decrease row every 4 rows 9 (11, 11, 13, 13) times

more—22 (24, 29, 31, 36) stitches remain.

Work even until the armhole measures 8½ (9, 9½, 10, 10½)" (21.5 [23, 24, 25.5, 26.5]cm). Bind off the remaining stitches.

## Left Front

Work the same as for the Right Front, reversing all shaping.

## Sleeves (Make 2)

With A and straight needles, cast on 58 (62, 62, 66, 66) stitches.

Work in the cuff rib pattern until the piece measures about 3" (7.5cm) from the cast-on edge, ending with a right-side row.

**NEXT ROW (WS):** Work in rib and increase 2 stitches evenly spaced across the row—60 (64, 64, 68, 68) stitches.

Begin the houndstooth pattern and increase at each side of every 4 rows 2 (2, 13, 16, 25) times, every 6 rows 15 (20, 12, 10, 4) times, then every 8 rows 4 (0, 0, 0, 0) times, working the new stitches in the houndstooth pattern—102 (108, 114, 120, 126) stitches.

Continue even in pattern until sleeve measures 24¾ (25, 25, 25½, 25¾)" (63 [63.5, 63.5, 65, 65.5]cm) from the cast-on. Bind off all stitches.

## Finishing

Weave in all the ends. Block all pieces to the finished measurements.

Sew the shoulder seams.

Sew the side and sleeve seams, using a 2-stitch seam allowance for a clean seam.

## Zipper Band and Collar

With A and right side facing, begin at lower left front, and pick up and knit 158 (163, 168, 173, 178) stitches along left front, 55 (57, 57, 59, 59) stitches across back neck, and 158 (163, 168, 173, 178) stitches along right front—371 (383, 393, 405, 415) stitches.

Beginning with Row 2, work in the zipper band rib pattern until band measures 2" (5cm), ending with a wrong-side row. Bind off all stitches in pattern.

Sew in the zipper with the top of the zipper at the beginning of the front neck shaping.

---

## MAKE IT MORE FEMININE *OR* MASCULINE

Substitute Navy (left) for black and skew this sweater even manlier. Cherry Red (right) transforms it into a gal's Chanel-inspired jacket. Consider leaving the zipper off if you're making this for a woman, and wearing it with a wide leather belt.

COLOR

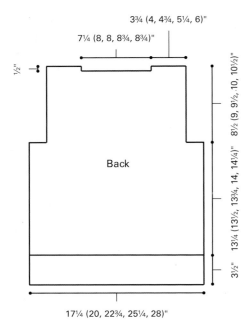

3¾ (4, 4¾, 5¼, 6)"

7¼ (8, 8, 8¾, 8¾)"

½"

8½ (9, 9½, 10, 10½)"

Back

13¼ (13½, 13¾, 14, 14¼)"

3½"

17¼ (20, 22¾, 25¼, 28)"

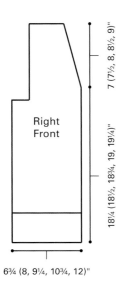

7 (7½, 8, 8½, 9)"

Right
Front

18¼ (18½, 18¾, 19, 19¼)"

6¾ (8, 9¼, 10¾, 12)"

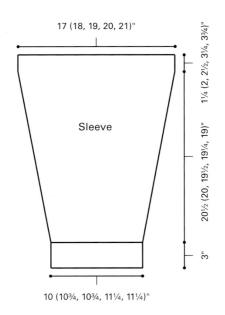

17 (18, 19, 20, 21)"

1¼ (2, 2½, 3¼, 3¾)"

Sleeve

20½ (20, 19½, 19¼, 19)"

3"

10 (10¾, 10¾, 11¼, 11¼)"

## HOUNDSTOOTH PATTERN

(mult 4 sts)

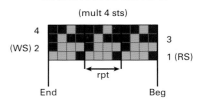

4

(WS) 2

3

1 (RS)

rpt

End                    Beg

### COLOR KEY

☐ = A

■ = B

### STITCH KEY

☐ = K on RS; p on WS

*Note: When increasing to shape the sleeve underarm edges, begin each row one stitch farther out from the repeat with each increase worked.*

# MY FATHER'S
## SWEATER

My father passed away during the spring semester of my sophomore year in college. It was unexpected and traumatic for the entire family. A few weeks afterward, Mom took some time out West with her dearest friend to recompose herself while I took up the task of organizing Dad's clothes for donations.

Mom had already put the winter sweaters in storage, a basement closet that smelled of heating oil and mothballs. I started here. It took hours to go through a small pile, each sweater releasing a flood of memories: Dad spilling wine on one sweater at my eighteenth birthday dinner at a narrow restaurant on Mulberry Street in Little Italy; Dad sitting next to me at a Bob Fosse musical wearing a sweater I had given him for Father's Day.

At the bottom of the closet was a sweater I didn't recognize. Confused, I tore open the yellowing dry cleaner's bag. This was clearly an old sweater, one I had never seen him wear, never knew he owned. It was an unstructured black alpaca blend cardigan, loosely knit with four buttons and a deep V-neck. There was no label and the seams looked hand-sewn. It was gorgeous and felt comfortable without the weight of my many memories. This one was not going to charity. I brought it out to the deck to air out for the afternoon.

That night, I called Mom and asked her about the black alpaca sweater.

"I made it for him for our honeymoon," she said.

I hung up, opened a beer, and sat down to hours of home movies, starting with their honeymoon, a tape I'd watched endlessly as a child. In every scene, from the parrot farm in Miami to the stroll along Ocean Drive in South Beach, there was that sweater, a little out of place in Florida, even if it was December. I couldn't believe I hadn't noticed it in all the years I'd watched this movie. Dad must have been overheated and itchy in all that alpaca, but his new wife had made it for him and he looked happy.

For years, I wore Dad's black alpaca sweater. It was not only my favorite wardrobe item, it was one of the nicest things in my closet. I wore it so often that the seams started to open and buttons needed replacing after a few years, but it was vintage and spectacular. An antique dealer, a tall, older woman in a shop on Christopher Street in Greenwich Village, once offered me anything in her shop I could carry out in exchange for the sweater. Not a chance.

Sadly, I left the sweater in a taxi about seven years later. The cab company said the driver never found it.

We wear other people's sweaters for many reasons. We're cold, and a friend gives us the shirt off his back. Or we like the way a sweater reminds us of the person it belongs to. Or we find one in a taxi and fall in love with it. I'm glad that black sweater found a third life, carrying a little piece of my dad, and me, with it. For the person who wore it after us, it contained no emotional weight, just the endless possibilities of who might have made it, who might have worn it, and who might wear it after them.

# Abbreviations

| | |
|---|---|
| **cn** | cable needle |
| **k** | knit |
| **k1b** | knit into the stitch in the row below; see "Shaker Rib Stitch, or Knitting One Below," p. 52 |
| **k2tog** | knit 2 together |
| **k3tog** | knit 3 together |
| **kfb** | knit in front and back of the stitch; detailed instructions p. 17. |
| **mult** | multiple |
| **p** | purl |
| **p2tog** | purl 2 together |
| **pfb** | purl in front and back of a stitch; detailed instructions p. 17. |
| **pm** | place marker |
| **rpt** | repeat |
| **rnd(s)** | round(s) |
| **RS** | right side |
| **ssk** | (slip, slip, knit) sl next 2 sts knitwise, one at a time, to right-hand needle, insert tip of left-hand needle into fronts of these sts, from left to right. Knit them together—1 stitch decreased. |
| **sssk** | (slip, slip, slip, knit) sl next 3 sts knitwise, one at a time, to right-hand needle, insert tip of left-hand needle into fronts of these sts from left to right. Knit them together—2 stitches decreased. |
| **ssp** | (slip, slip, purl) sl next 2 sts purlwise, one at a time, to right-hand needle, insert tip of left-hand needle into fronts of these sts, from left to right. Knit them tog—1 st decreased. |
| **st(s)** | stitch(es) |
| **tbl** | through back loop |
| **tog** | together |
| **WS** | wrong side |
| **yo** | yarn over |

# Yarn Guide

**Berroco, Inc.**
14 Elmdale Road
PO Box 367
Uxbridge, MA 01569
(800) 343-4948
www.berroco.com

**Blue Sky Alpacas, Inc.**
PO Box 88
Cedar, MN 55011
(888) 460-8862
www.blueskyalpacas.com

**Brooklyn Tweed**
85 York Street; 2nd Floor
Portland, ME 04101
(347) 878-9665
www.brooklyntweed.net

**Cascade Yarns**
1224 Andover Park East
Tukwila, WA 98188
(206) 574-0440
www.cascadeyarns.com

**Handknitting.com**
PO Box 10279
Jackson, WY 83002
(307) 200-0733
www.handknitting.com

**Karabella Yarns, Inc**
1201 Broadway
New York, NY 10001
(800) 550-0898
www.karabellayarns.com

**Knit One Crochet Too**
91 Tandberg Trail #6,
Windham, ME 04062
(800) 357-7646
www.knitonecrochettoo.com

**Kollage Yarns**
3591 Cahaba Beach Road
Birmingham, AL 35242
(888) 829-7758
www.kollageyarns.com

**Lion Brand Yarn Company**
34 West 15th Street
New York, NY 10011
(212) 243-8995
www.lionbrand.com

**Louet North America**
3425 Hands Road
Prescott, ON, Canada K0E1T0
(613) 925-4502 / (800) 897-6444
www.louet.com

**Manos Del Uruguay**
(Distributed by Fairmount Fibers
Ltd.)
915 N. 28th St.
Philadelphia, PA 19130
(888) 566-9970
www.fairmountfibers.com

**Rowan Yarns**
(Distributed by Westminster Fibers)
165 Ledge Street
Nashua, NH 03060
(800) 445-9276
www.knitrowan.com

**Shibui Knits, LLC.**
1500 NW 18th, Suite 110
Portland, OR 97209
(503) 595-5898.
www.shibuiknits.com

**Supreme Possum Merino**
(Available at Handknitting.com)
47 Craigleith St.
Dunedin
New Zealand
027-3165-885
www.merinopossum.co.nz

**Zitron Gobi**
(Distributed by Skacel Collection,
Inc.)
PO Box 88110
Seattle, WA 98138
(800) 255-1278
www.skacelknitting.com

# Standard Yarn Weight System

| CYCA | 1 | 2 | 3 | 4 | 5 |
|---|---|---|---|---|---|
| Yarn Weight | Lace, Fingering, Sock | Sport | DK, Light Worsted | Worsted, Aran | Chunky |
| Average Knit Gauge over 4" (10cm)* | 27–32sts | 23–26 sts | 21–24 sts | 16–20 sts | 12–15 sts |
| Recommended Needle in US Size Range | 1–3 | 3–5 | 5–7 | 7–9 | 9–11 |
| Recommended Needle in Metric Size Range | 2.25–3.25mm | 3.25–3.75mm | 3.75–4.5mm | 4.5–5.5mm | 5.5–8mm |

* Guidelines only: The chart reflects the most commonly used gauges and needle sizes for specific yarn categories. Always follow the gauge stated in your pattern.

## KEEPING TRACK OF ROWS

Row counters are terrific gadgets but be careful: Some have a tendency to advance on their own inside a knitting bag. Look for one that has a locking feature so the numbers can't change without you. Another nice choice is an electronic counter, especially one that you can download to your smart phone so you can track numerous projects at once. If you're going at it old-school and making hash marks in the margins of your pattern, do them in pencil. You can erase them when you're done and be ready to go the next time you make that sweater.

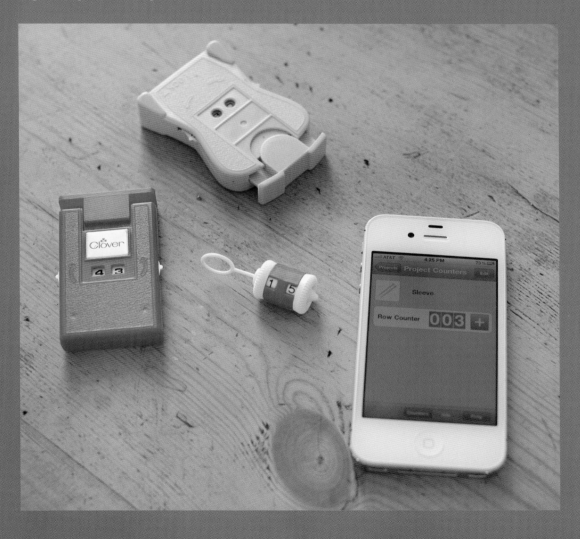

# Project Index

Off-Center Half-Zip Mock
Turtle (page 24)

Oversized Turtleneck
(page 28)

Color Block Jersey (page 35)

Camel Cabled Cardigan (page 40)

Shaker Cardigan (page 54)

Linen Scarf or Wrap (page 61)

Seed Placket Pullover
(page 64)

Textured Argyle Cardigan
(page 70)

Honeycomb Pullover (page 75)

Reversible Cable Scarf (page 88)

Double-Knit Double-Knot Scarf (page 90)

Reversible Paisley Hat (page 95)

Boat Neck Faux Rib Pullover (page 98)

Reversible Herringbone Scarf (page 103)

Varsity Sweater (page 115)

Funnel Neck Pullover with Raglan Details (page 126)

Fair Isle Cardigan (page 131)

Plaid Pullover (page 138)

Houndstooth Cardigan (page 145)

# Index